Professor Glyn Davis is Professor of Political Science and Vice-Chancellor at the University of Melbourne.

Boyer Lectures

Each year the ABC invites a prominent Australian to present the result of his or her work and thinking on major social, scientific or cultural issues in a series of radio talks known as the Boyer Lectures. The series was inaugurated in 1959 under the title of ABC Lectures, but in 1961 was renamed as a memorial to the late Sir Richard Boyer who, as chairman of the ABC, had been one of those responsible for its introduction.

Visit abc.net.au/rn/boyerlectures for further information and for a complete list of Boyer Lecture speakers.

GLYN DAVIS

The Republic of Learning

The Boyer Lectures are broadcast each year on ABC Radio National and are available at abc.net.au/rn/boyerlectures. ABC Radio National is available throughout Australia on 260 transmitters including:

Adelaide 729AM
Brisbane 792AM
Canberra 846AM
Darwin 657AM
Gold Coast 90.1FM
Hobart 585AM
Melbourne 621AM
Newcastle 1512AM
Perth 810AM
Sydney 576AM

For your local frequency go to the ABC Radio National website at abc.net.au/rn or call 1300 13 9994 during working hours. Listen online at abc.net.au/rn

For ABC Radio National broadcast times and program details go to abc.net.au/rn or call Radio National listener enquiries on 02 8333 2821 during working hours.

GLYN DAVIS

The Republic of Learning

Boyer Lecture Series 2010

ABC
Books

The ABC 'Wave' device is a trademark of the Australian Broadcasting Corporation and is used under licence by HarperCollins*Publishers* Australia.

First published in Australia in 2010
by HarperCollins*Publishers* Australia Pty Limited
ABN 36 009 913 517
harpercollins.com.au

HarperCollins*Publishers*
25 Ryde Road, Pymble, Sydney, NSW 2073, Australia
31 View Road, Glenfield, Auckland 0627, New Zealand
A 53, Sector 57, Noida, UP, India
77–85 Fulham Palace Road, London, W6 8JB, United Kingdom
2 Bloor Street East, 20th floor, Toronto, Ontario M4W 1A8, Canada
10 East 53rd Street, New York NY 10022, USA

National Library of Australia Cataloguing-in-Publication data

Davis, Glyn.
    The republic of learning : higher education transforms Australia / Glyn Davis.
    ISBN: 978 0 7333 2874 9 (pbk.)
    Education, Higher–Aims and objectives–Australia.
    Universities and colleges–Australia.
    Universities and colleges–Sociological aspects.
378.994

Cover design by Mark Thacker
Cover images by shutterstock.com
Typeset in Sabon 10.5/15.5pt by Letter Spaced
Printed and bound in Australia by Griffin Press
70gsm Classic used by HarperCollins*Publishers* is a natural, recyclable product made
from wood grown in sustainable forests. The manufacturing processes conform to the
environmental regulations in the country of origin, Finland.

7 6 5 4 3 2 1   10 11 12 13 14

contents

For Margaret

One
The Global Moment

Ego mundi civis esse cupio wrote Erasmus to a friend in 1522 — 'I should like to be a citizen of the world'.

So he proved.

Erasmus of Rotterdam was arguably the first modern global citizen. He was neither statesman nor soldier, not an artist but an intellectual. More precisely, Erasmus was an academic.

Erasmus was the best-known international thinker of his era — far more famous in his moment than today's celebrated professors.

'Prolific' does not quite do Erasmus justice. In the 1530s he wrote perhaps a fifth of all books sold in the world.

Like other popular thinkers, Erasmus displayed a gift for expressing ideas simply. He is credited with saying, 'In the land of the blind, the one-eyed man is king'. He reworked Pliny to urge, 'Live as if you are to die tomorrow, study as if you were to live forever'. Many students obey the first clause — the best heed both.

At fewer than 140 characters, both sayings would fit easily in the flowing river of Twitter.

Yet, while an extraordinary thinker, Erasmus was just the best-known of an impressive network of academics who corresponded and travelled between the great universities of the then known world — Oxford, Cambridge, Padua, the Sorbonne, and private academies in those cradles of classical education Florence, Venice and Rome.

In her 2009 Mann Booker Prize-winning novel *Wolf Hall*, Hilary Mantel portrays the friendship between Erasmus and the one he famously dubbed 'a man for all seasons' — the churchman, lawyer, philosopher and statesman Sir Thomas More. Erasmus once wrote an entire book, *In Praise of Folly*, in just a week, to amuse his friend More. But theirs was also a world in which ideas were taken seriously — and had consequences. Thomas More, famously, lost his head for refusing to bend convictions to political imperative.

These thinkers were by no means exclusively from an economic elite or ruling class. Thomas More was wealthy, and became Lord Chancellor of England — the prime minister of his time. Yet the pattern of the sixteenth century shows that smart boys from humble backgrounds — it was centuries before the same privilege extended to women — could win scholarships and enter this glittering circle. Erasmus was the illegitimate child of a trainee priest and a doctor's daughter — not particularly highly paid professions back then, but callings that took education seriously. Though in his teens Erasmus lost both parents to plague, he had the good fortune to be educated in schools and monasteries renowned for their commitment to learning.

We know the appearance of these men because More, Erasmus and many others had their portraits painted by leading artists of their day, including Holbein the Younger. Each typically is shown in his study, surrounded by books in Latin and Greek.

This clue suggests two important characteristics in these intellectuals: they saw themselves as part of a conversation through correspondence in shared scholarly languages, and they were the first generation of westerners to live entirely in the age of the printing press.

Armed with new thinking, and new communications, Erasmus and his contemporaries aspired to be citizens of the world. And though it remained a man's world, some women participated through sheer brilliance and force of character. Margaret, daughter of Thomas More, was regarded as the most intelligent woman in England — like her near-contemporary Queen Elizabeth I, highly admired for her Greek and Latin composition.

We know Erasmus and his contemporary group of scholars as the republic of letters.

The term was drawn from *respublica litteraria*, which might translate as 'commonwealth of learning' or perhaps 'commonwealth of scholars' — a group of people who saw themselves as intellectual equals, committed to sharing knowledge. By circulating their letters and books to sympathetic audiences, by discussing new ideas and developing a critical apparatus for assessing claims to knowledge, these leading thinkers in Europe created a conversation outside the usual constraints of nationality and censorship. They inhabited an 'imagined community', a world in which scholars conversed through writing.

The metaphor of a republic of letters was taken seriously and often literally. Learned academies were established across Europe, to receive and discuss the letters carrying new learning. Just as scholars were concerned to establish rules of evidence, so these academies invented elaborate rules to shape and govern exchanges. They may be regarded, suggests historian Peter Burke, as 'so many mini-republics, each with its own written constitution'.

Like republics, the learned academies prided themselves on being self-governing, and were zealous about independence from worldly power. They were places of debate and disagreement — but places where equal citizens practised intellectual freedom.

And the result?

As one of the leading historians of this movement — Cambridge University's Quentin Skinner — argues, the republic of letters helped 'initiate an intellectual revolution which eventually led to the overthrow of scholasticism'.

Which is to say, it replaced a way of thinking based on revealed truth with one grounded in rational inquiry. So, for instance, while scholastics accepted Plato's teaching that the earth lay at the centre of a series of spheres, members of the new republic of letters used mathematics, systematic observation and later new instruments such as the quadrant and telescope to explore the actual movement of the heavenly bodies.

Before this republic of letters, the few universities in Europe were remote, monastic and contemplative organisations, focused on a limited store of ancient texts. Through their own structures and activities, universities expressed the Aristotelian ideal of a divinely ordered universe whose hierarchy was reflected in society itself.

Erasmus and his generation challenged this idea of scholarship as the exposition of revealed truth. The republic of letters instead encouraged universities to become lively, questioning institutions, concerned less with arid abstract contemplation and more with how we should live. They created self-conscious communities where students and scholars explored new learning, operating through formal rules that encouraged argument, evidence and controversy and became, in time, the basis of scientific method.

Every new idea has a history. The European humanists in turn drew on rich contributions to scholarship from Indian, Chinese and Arab thinkers. The long-established universities of the Arab world made significant contributions to mathematics and astronomy, preserving as well the Greek classics that inspired the humanists.

In the following centuries, universities would contribute to the scientific and industrial revolutions. And while much was invented by people who worked outside the campus, many were informed by a way of thinking first expressed in letters and lectures.

The Republic of Learning

The republic of letters was a forerunner to our world, the first intimation of one of those rare moments in humanity — as a character says in Tom Stoppard's *Arcadia* — when the door is kicked open and a new world revealed.

* * *

Five hundred years later there is a new exchange underway, once again across borders and languages, a sharing of ideas and people on an unprecedented scale. It is the modern world of higher education — the republic of learning.

We might think of the republican ideal as merely the absence of a monarch. But in classical and Renaissance times it meant so much more.

Republics were understood as one of the crowning glories of human invention — settings for freedom in which people could pursue the humanist goal of perfectibility — of our intellect, culture and social relations.

Republics were not always democratic in the modern sense, but they treated their citizens equally and respected the rule of law. They developed a notion of civic virtue that placed the public good above the private.

Republics accepted disagreement as a necessary part of the human condition, the only way citizens can understand their options and make an informed choice.

Republics invented institutions to ventilate and resolve differences, recognising in the words of English constitutional writer Walter Bagehot, that 'no State can be first-rate which has not a government by discussion'.

Republics were fiercely independent islands in seas of tyranny and conformity. And given this commitment to competition of ideas, they accepted diversity as essential.

Monarchies may be centralised and uniform, understood by their gaps and silences. In a republic, as Alexis de Tocqueville said of early America, no elite or metropolis prevailed, but rather 'the intelligence and power of the people are disseminated through all the parts of this vast country, and instead of radiating from a common point they cross each other in every direction'.

And as with ancient Rome, republics were restless, ambitious, outward-looking, global in orientation, keen to conquer the blue skies. They wanted to share their innovations in law, philosophy, culture and society with the world.

Erasmus and his contemporaries put these principles to work and changed their world. They inspired later generations to cast an even wider net of ideas, extending their conversation across the Atlantic.

The original republic of letters saw a handful of intellectuals converse through languages understood by just a minuscule proportion of the population, via monographs produced on hand-operated printing presses. By contrast, today's republic of learning is vast in scale, with a membership in the hundreds of millions.

No longer donkeys and round-bottomed ships to transport scholars and their books at sailing pace.

No longer languages of the few — Latin and Greek — but English, Spanish and Mandarin, in a global society aspiring to worldwide literacy.

For handwritten letters that took weeks to arrive, now the immediacy of email.

For Gutenberg's press and moveable type, now the internet and personal computers: whole libraries, compressed centuries of learning, available instantly.

This republic of learning spans the planet, shaping every nation including our own.

In Australia, going to university, once unusual, has become a standard expectation for young people. More than a million Australian and international students study this year in our university system, and nearly twice that number again in vocational and technical education.

In many metropolitan and regional centres, universities and technical colleges are the largest local employers — sometimes rivalled only by hospitals, themselves often allied to university medical schools.

The knowledge and the skills provided by higher learning help drive the extraordinary increases in wealth Australians have enjoyed in recent decades. Graduates locate minerals in the Kimberley, staff our advanced medical services design our transport networks, spin the wheels of finance, advise government ministers, regulate industries, analyse social trends, produce the movies, theatre, television, books and small magazines that trace our national preoccupations.

Researchers in our republic of learning discover new knowledge, opening further possibilities for humanity. From advances in health that improve life expectancy to insights in political economy that encourage more affluent and socially just societies, from inventions in information technology to speed up *use of capital – neoliberal market concept*

global communications to the insights of climate scientists that might just prove crucial for survival on this planet, university research contributes to understanding and innovation.

Higher learning gives us the human capital to ensure future prosperity — and the cultural capital to find greater meaning in our lives.

This enthusiastic involvement in the republic of learning is replicated across the world. A handful of humanists in the time of Erasmus has grown to more than 150 million higher education students and staff worldwide.

The small flocks of adventurous scholars making intellectual pilgrimages between England, Italy, France and the German states have become around 3.5 million students travelling abroad to study every year.

The university has become a familiar institution, reproduced thousands of times around the globe, mini-republics each claiming independence from the societies around them, committed to truth and knowledge as universal values, to be identified through shared standards of scholarship.

This new global reality gives students unprecedented opportunities to study in other places, to mix with people from different cultures, to rise above the surly bonds of place — to do what learning does best: allow us each to break the narrow prison of self and understand worlds beyond our direct experience.

The expansion of higher education — this republic of learning — makes knowledge available to an audience wider than any previously imagined. It encourages global mobility of people and ideas.

One by-product is a huge world trade in higher education, worth more than $35 billion a year in English-speaking countries alone.

And who guessed Australia would prove among the most successful providers of higher education in the world? Despite our small number of institutions, some 7 per cent of the world's international students choose to study in Australia. They find quality universities, welcoming cities and truly international campuses: with one in five students at every Australian university drawn from overseas, we host the most internationalised higher education system in the world.

Whether these international students ultimately return home or stay to make a life in Australia, they engage with our nation and carry that experience through their lives. The benefits for our nation are vast, if intangible. At a meeting last year in Kuala Lumpur with Malaysian ministers, I asked everyone about their education, and was pleasantly surprised to discover a majority were graduates of an Australian university — and inclined, hopefully, to warm and closer relations between our nations.

Few appreciate just how much Australia's current prosperity rests on this new export industry called education. International students spend $3.7 billion every year at Australia's thirty-seven public and two private universities.

For every dollar an international student invests in learning, they spend another two on services, accommodation, food and entertainment while living in Australia. There are businesses and families across this land, far from the world of education, whose livelihood and prospects depend on the global trade in education. For them, Australia rides on the scholar's back.

Universities have become one of the world's major incentives for people movement. They act as magnets for those in search of new opportunity, much like the goldfields or rich pastures did in nineteenth-century Australia. As Ben Wildavsky noted in *The Great Brain Race*, universities have become part of the international competition for talent, for innovation, for renewal.

Visionaries and reformers talked for decades about opening up our once insular, provincial, protectionist and 'lucky' island nation. Higher education has proved a big part of that change. It happened quickly. Hardly anyone noticed at first. Yet look around and see its mighty works.

The flow of students has made Australia a global destination. The most recent RMIT index, measuring the world's most lively, diverse and intellectually vibrant urban centres, ranks London, Boston and Tokyo the great international cities — followed immediately by Melbourne and Sydney, significantly ahead of Paris, New York, Berlin and Hong Kong.

As we debate population matters, we should be careful to keep this precious new knowledge industry strong. The invisible hand of student spending shapes our cities, brings the world to our table, keeps Australia affluent, connected — and young.

The traffic flows both ways. Thousands of young Australians experience study abroad as part of their university courses, sharpening their languages skills, developing empathy for the cultures of Asia and beyond, building links that will serve through their lives.

In any week, Australian alumni will gather somewhere — lawyers in Shanghai, accountants in London, artists in Singapore, marine biologists in San Diego. Those graduates are harbingers of an emerging Australia, at home in the world and our region. It is far more difficult to maintain a closed society when so many of the leaders have wider horizons.

Look at the faces in the street, the lecture hall, the library — students who study in large public universities and numerous private colleges, who live around their campuses, who bring youth and vitality to our cities. Drawn from everywhere, international students help create, and enjoy, the diverse, tolerant, enriched society Australia has long promised. These young people are our single largest source of new citizens. They are the generation that will in time make our society truly global.

The benefits are more than economic. What happens in our universities helps us live longer, reduces the tyranny of distance and time, provides insight into the nature of the universe itself. Thanks to higher education, we too live in an era when the door is kicked open and we can glimpse what awaits beyond.

* * *

For students, the growth of a global system of higher education has opened opportunities for people young and old to study abroad, to seek new knowledge through online courses, to share in the contest of ideas at the heart of campus life.

Nation states too have come to value universities as sources of skilled professionals, research and invention. For many nations, building great universities has become a mark of their global competitiveness. The current investment in new facilities in China and the Middle East is beyond anything in human history. Whole new settlements are being designed around universities.

In southern China, the Guangzhou University City is a new education precinct containing ten university campuses spread over more than 18 square kilometres. This is just the first stage — eventually, authorities hope, 200,000 students and 20,000 academic staff will live and study in this planned community.

In September 2009 the Saudi government opened the King Abdullah University of Science and Technology — a 36 square kilometre complex by the Red Sea. With a $10 billion endowment, this co-educational university is designed to build Saudi strength in research. The king at the opening ceremony said: 'The Islamic nation knows too well that it will not be powerful unless it depends on, after God, science.'

There is more construction underway on campuses across the world than ever before. The global competition for students and staff has become fierce and unrelenting.

Universities are forming international associations, seeding new campuses abroad, simultaneously treating each other as equals and desperately competing across the planet. Institutions are crossing borders, becoming multinational, operating in many places but owned by none. For the first time ever such institutions can be compared and graded in a global ranking system, so creating an international hierarchy of status.

Yet change is always creative *and* destructive. Just as the birth of the republic of letters spelt the end of the medieval university system, the technologies that allow universities to become global institutions also test the familiar style of campus education. As the web makes knowledge widely available, so it undercuts the traditional authority of professors. What was once largely a public or not-for-profit activity has attracted large and successful private competitors. Mail-order courses always existed on the margins of higher learning, but the combination of new technology and sophisticated private provision has created commercial phenomena such as the private University of Phoenix. These global enterprises package for a worldwide market programs once offered only by traditional public universities.

As new humanist academies arose in the sixteenth century to challenge the scholastic institutions, so new forms of learning confront received wisdom about what a university is, what it does and how it works.

The effects will be far-reaching but unpredictable. Even as it opens new possibilities, change undermines existing institutions, challenges regulatory frameworks, upsets our expectations of the world. The growth of international networks and global competition subvert a national approach to education and upset everything we think we know about higher learning.

What emerges is a new republic of learning — a dense global universe of institutions, providers and websites, competing products and educational philosophies, all seeking to package knowledge, share it widely, and sometimes profit from it.

Older standards of prestige and authority, of universities as gatekeepers of knowledge, are called into question by this new world.

* * *

As the importance of higher learning increases, this seems the right time to consider the republic of learning and, with it, the prospects for our nation in an age of knowledge.

Though the focus on these chapters will be on universities — the institutions I know best — it is impossible to consider higher learning without acknowledging the vocational and technical colleges, private providers, and international campuses that share the post-school education mission across this nation.

In the chapters to follow, we will explore this new world of higher learning: the centrality of teaching, the rise of research, the difficult question of who gets to be a citizen of the republic of learning, life on campus, and the policy questions for a sector that is nationally based but increasingly global in outlook.

The tone will be optimistic — universities are reasserting their role as centres for thinking, and doing so with unprecedented reach and significance. They have become vital to national economic growth, to the life chances and potential happiness of every Australian.

And universities remain the most extraordinary places to study and work: fascinating amalgams of medieval customs and modern management. They have become the inspiration for the most successful global companies, such as Google, which build campuses instead of factories or offices, arrange staff in the loose structures of university departments, and compete with graduate schools for the best and the brightest.

We will trace the evolution of the modern university as it builds on the values that animated the original republic of letters inspired by Erasmus half a millennium ago.

Niccolò Machiavelli, among the greatest theorists of republicanism, understood republics in his day as highly imperfect states, always in flux. Each republic was unique, hard to govern, sometimes chaotic, yet with characteristics that made it worth defending: in a sea of despotism, reaction and intellectual conformity, the republics of Machiavelli's time were islands of equality, freedom, progress, choice and genius. Their achievements set the pace for the rest of humanity.

Stagnation was always the true enemy. Complacency and success in a society are the enemies of innovation. Stagnation can result when communities seek to constrain knowledge for cultural, economic or religious reasons. Excessive regulation can prove a major obstacle.

And stagnation can happen inside the academy. So these lectures will celebrate diversity. There is no single best model for a university, no gold standard despite the impression promoted by global rankings. A society does best when it has access to diversity and specialisation — to a lively and contesting set of voices offering very different philosophies of higher education.

Hence we will close by asking where to from here — what policy choices will ensure the republic of learning delivers for

Australia its extraordinary potential? Will Australians make the investment necessary to reap the rich harvest of knowledge, skills and culture that awaits us?

* * *

Just as every university is both ancient and modern, traditional and innovative, so the original proponents of the republic of letters believed in change and preservation. ✗

Progress, they argued, is constructed on the achievements of the past. Erasmus sought to reform the corrupt church of his time, but recognised that change also offers temptation to zealotry, immoderation, intolerance and shallowness. He saw change for change's sake as an enemy of the good society or of any hope to build a better one. Erasmus sought to conserve as well as improve and so, apparently paradoxically, he became a reformer who opposed full-scale church reformation. His powers of reasoning told him there were aspects of the old church worth retaining.

It is a spirit worth emulating as we consider higher education. Much needs to be done that is new — but much needs to be preserved.

The constants of learning — wide-ranging curiosity, questioning, rigour in the search for truth and knowledge — must remain guiding principles in a new republic of learning. They ensure universities remain more than skill factories.

Some mistakenly believe that students only apply to university as their way to a job; the rest of the campus experience is nothing but drinking beer.

Observation strongly suggests otherwise. Yes, universities produce 'knowledge workers'. Their contribution to human capital and national productivity is important and can be measured.

Yet time at university is cherished because it is about more than getting a job. Not everyone will live in college, perform in student theatre, run for office in the student union, join the debating competition or study abroad. But everyone who leaves a university with a qualification — and sometimes without — is touched forever by the experience. They're no better than anyone else, but they are equipped with training to interrogate and understand the world. Graduates have been exposed to a universal culture that values the intellect as something worthwhile in its own right. They are recognisably the heirs of Erasmus and More, members of an invisible but shared republic of learning.

How this spirit is imparted through teaching will be the subject of the next chapter.

Ego mundi civis esse cupio. It is a noble ambition, now possible thanks to a global movement of people and ideas. To be a citizen of the world is the promise of the republic of learning.

Two
A Lectern in a Dusty Room

Come a weekend each August, universities around Australia throw open the gates. Months of preparation converge on Open Day. Volunteers are trained, publications readied, tents hired, corridors polished, lawns trimmed, displays prepared.

Are sufficient information sessions booked? Will the campus radio station have enough guests to keep its programs lively? What happens if we run out of leaflets? Will people find the psychology department up there on the tenth floor? Why do we persist in holding this annual event in the coldest, wettest month of the year?

And most worrying of all, what if no one turns up?

But every year the crowds arrive, early and eager — those still in secondary school, thinking about their future, parents and friends anxious about career possibilities, those older and thinking about taking a degree, graduates interested in returning to study, the curious, the cynical and the enthusiastic.

Some 17,000 visitors explored the Bentley campus of Curtin University in Western Australia this year. Nova FM broadcast on-site, while academics offered information sessions from morning until dusk. There were food stalls, book displays, an art exhibition, a 'name the fossil' contest in applied geology, and a 'longest throw' competition to demonstrate the measurement skills of surveyors.

La Trobe University in Victoria not only organised separate Open Days for each of its campuses at Mildura, Shepparton, Albury-Wodonga and Bendigo, but offered a La Trobe roadshow to reach people as far afield as Broken Hill, the Riverland and the Mallee.

The University of Adelaide Open Day promised visitors a full day of activities, with lectures from every faculty, advice on life skills, and an intriguing session titled 'Pigs, Foam and Fishing: The life of a petroleum engineer'.

The University of Canberra offered campus tours all day, inviting prospective students to see accommodation options.

For those unable to attend Open Day at Monash in Melbourne, information sessions were streamed on the university website.

Across the country, Open Days remind us of the wealth of possibilities on every campus. Staff put in long hours answering questions, offering sample lectures. Student guides hand out balloons and show off the amenities — not just impressive libraries and laboratories but the sports grounds, theatres, food halls and colleges that are part of the university experience.

When the student union organised a protest at one university Open Day, the march and placards were applauded warmly by the crowds, apparently mistaking them for another staged exhibit of campus life.

Open Day emphasises choice — the vast array of courses available at every university. It invites potential students to decide which branch of knowledge will capture their imagination — and their future.

When they start their studies, students encounter the oldest and still core part of university life — learning and teaching, the transmission not just of ideas but of the methods to explore and discover for themselves. Learning and teaching delivers the intellectual frameworks through which we understand the world, think about great and important ideas, assimilate new information, and in turn make a contribution. The best learning on campus involves 'practical chemistry' — a process that changes teacher and student alike.

This chapter explores the enterprise of learning and teaching. Study at university is never a settled question, but always restless and on the move. There is endless debate about the best teaching methods, the most appropriate curriculum. This affirms the importance of diversity in our higher education system. Students should be able to choose among many different approaches to teaching. The republic of learning works best amid constant experimentation, lively competition, a nagging worry that somewhere, somehow, there must be even better ways to share knowledge.

* * *

The academy has long been marked by disputes about how to teach. The very first recorded republic of learning, the Academy of Plato in classical Athens — where Aristotle was a student — engaged in strident scholarly conflict. Its opponents were a rival school, the Sophists. Debate centred on what should be taught. The Platonists favoured philosophy and mathematics, while the Sophists emphasised the skills of rhetoric and persuasion.

At stake were contending visions about the nature of knowledge.

Such differences survive to the present day. They are central to what we teach and how it is presented. Should students approach a discipline through case studies, as in many business schools, or start with theory? Is it best to get design students early into the studio, or first to build conceptual foundations? Do we stress breadth over depth, student choice or required courses?

There are highly plausible, but diametrically opposed, answers to each of these questions. People learn differently, and finding an approach that works for everyone is difficult. There are engineering degrees that begin by taking apart a small toy robot to examine its design, and engineering programs that start with classes in advanced maths and physics. Some do both.

A masters degree in architecture at the University of Melbourne asks new students to build the corner of a small house, from foundation to roof, on the lawn of the architecture school. The challenge is to translate a construction drawing into physical form. There are only limited materials available and the students must meet the design intent while managing the technical complexities of bringing several materials together correctly as they turn a corner.

Required to finish in time for Open Day, students who may never before have laboured with their hands must work against the clock, under the watchful eye of fellow students, to build a watertight shelter from the fixed supply of materials assembled, in the correct order.

The lessons learned, suggests the course convener — about sequencing, about the virtue of simplicity, about what materials can and cannot do — influence everything the students subsequently design.

How we teach changes regularly. *What* we teach is part tradition, part response to emerging fields of knowledge, and part industrial practice to control entry to a profession. Though architecture may be an ancient craft, faculties of architecture did not emerge at Australian universities until the 1920s. The list of careers requiring tertiary education is not fixed, but fluid and often contested.

Nursing, for example, was traditionally taught within hospitals. The move to university training, beginning in Australia in the 1980s and not completed until 1993, proved highly contentious. As one nurse recalled, 'The degree holders were given hell by the profession'. Many felt strongly that nursing is a calling that must be learned firsthand in the wards.

Those who pressed for tertiary qualifications argued that nursing had become too demanding and complex to remain outside formal education. Nurses now embrace responsibilities once reserved for doctors, from triage decisions about incoming patients to administering IV antibiotics and inserting cannulae. To be part of medical teams, nurses need expertise and professional standing, something secured through university education. Indeed some forms of nursing have become so highly specialised that they are only taught at postgraduate level.

To support this new level of professionalism, nursing has developed a research agenda. Academics in nursing pursue doctoral level study, and produce peer-reviewed publications, across every aspect of nursing practice. The result is an ever-growing body of knowledge to share with students.

The story of nursing can be told about many fields, reflecting more complex workplaces and job descriptions. Universities have come to monopolise professional training. Around two-thirds of Australian university students study in professional courses, from actuarial studies to veterinary science. Whole traditions of knowledge once handed down through apprenticeships or on-the-job training have been captured in textbooks, translated into university courses, structured into semesters and exam questions.

Often the imperative is simply the explosion of information. The knowledge expected in most disciplines has expanded beyond recognition and must somehow be compressed into relatively short degrees. One professor of nursing estimates that 'we fit into a semester almost the whole of the learning in my three-year hospital-based program of 1975'.

The need to cover so much detail has inspired new thinking about university education.

Walk around campus on Open Day, and there is much that seems familiar — lecture halls, laboratories and tutorial rooms, a large library or two, glasshouses for the botany students, water tanks for marine science demonstrations, theatre spaces for the drama class, a moot court room for budding lawyers in which to hone their presentations.

Much basic teaching is still done through lectures, that traditional if not always effective way to speak to large groups of students — lecture from *lectus*, the act of reading.

Yet students also spend time in tutorials discussing ideas, clustered in groups around workbenches with screens and electronic microscopes, working together using collaborative software to solve a puzzle.

And even in the lecture theatre, the best teachers do not just read aloud from notes. They profess, stimulate, provoke. They respond to student interest, take evasive action when boredom threatens. Good lecturers excite students about a topic, and inspire them to take part in the field, opening the door to futures they had not considered.

For some lecturers, the spoken word alone can convey their meaning and stimulate imaginations. Others supplement the classroom with the possibilities offered by technology — PowerPoint for the presentation, and for further study, web access to a wealth of background reading, multimedia materials, exercises and online discussion.

To ensure access for revision, every lecture is filmed and streamed. Students can compare and contrast — similar courses from other universities are available online. A lecturer on justice in Australia competes with Michael Sandel's course from Harvard, broadcast to the world. MIT makes available online the materials for every course it offers. The University of California Berkeley offers audio feeds from dozens of popular courses each semester.

Technology is no substitute for quality teaching, but it can create a richer classroom experience. Providing material online also reflects the practical circumstances of students. The average Australian university student attends classes for around thirteen hours each week, with more study time on campus or at home. Only 40 per cent of students receive some financial assistance from government or their institutions, so most must work at least part-time to support their study.

Since employment means time on campus is precious, electronic learning resources have become fundamental to university study. They link students to their teachers even when not there in person. Some universities go further, putting whole courses into distance-learning format so students can combine campus study with subjects accessed from afar.

This leads some to speculate the traditional university is not long for this world. 'Thirty years from now,' said management consultant Peter Drucker in 1997, 'the big university campuses will be relics. Universities won't survive. It's as large a change as when we first got the printed book.'

Is Drucker right — does traditional teaching on campus have a future? It is a question that nags many academics. To quote William Clark from his memorable *Academic Charisma and the Origins of the Research University*:

Anyone who has ever taught at a college or university must have had this experience. You're in the middle of something that you do every day: standing at a lectern in a dusty room … lecturing to a roomful of teenagers above whom hang almost visible clouds of hormones … Suddenly, you find yourself wondering … how you can possibly be doing this. Why, in the age of the World Wide Web, do professors still stand at podiums and blather for fifty minutes at unruly mobs of students, their lowered baseball caps imperfectly concealing the sleep buds that rim their eyes? Why do professors and students put on polyester gowns and funny hats and march, once a year … These activities seem both bizarre and disconnected, from one another and from modern life …

Yet there are reasons to doubt the imminent death of the familiar university. As Australian higher education analyst Gavin Moodie argues, learning remains very much a human activity, social as well as academic. There are reasons to get together on a campus, even to wear funny gowns. We need the firsthand experience of working with great teachers, of seeing how they approach knowledge, how 'learning as doing' informs their own scholarship.

Classrooms encourage focus and concentration. We learn by talking with other students as well as teachers, from non-visual cues, from 'aha!' moments as a teacher carries us to a new thought. Tutorials help nail points we had not understood and revisit ideas we overlooked. Group discussion reminds us that knowledge is always an argument about evidence — we need to hear a range of viewpoints, including those we will not accept.

Higher education offers training in analysis. It achieves this through discussion with teachers and fellow students. Along the way we learn to recognise poor arguments and faulty logic.

And, inevitably, we learn skills that are not on the formal curriculum, but still an essential part of education. When teaching about the European settlement of Australia, and the consequences for Indigenous peoples, a historian conveys what is known and what must remain conjecture. Implicit in the lesson is a demonstration of how to weigh contending evidence when the historical record is incomplete.

Likewise, there are medical skills learned through observation and immersion. Medical diagnosis relies on textbook knowledge, but how to choose from a vast repertoire of potential problems when seeing a patient? Medical students spend time with experienced clinicians, watching how they examine a sick person, the clues they seek, the subtle tricks of skilled diagnosis — closing the door to check for the characteristic odours of some ailments, walking around the room to see if the patient's eyes can track the doctor.

Following an experienced clinician on her rounds, seeing how she makes judgements, is an essential part of training. It is no wonder conversations between small groups of students and experienced doctors about a patient remain an important part of every medical program.

Technology will become an integral part of classroom

learning rather than a replacement. It allows innovative teachers to broaden a course, and students to participate in innovative ways. At the University of Queensland's TC Beirne School of Law, videoconferencing allows students to participate in an 'international' classroom, sharing their learning with peers across the world.

At the University of Wollongong, Dr Karen Daly teaches Spanish through short online exercises. As a specialist in Medieval Spanish literature, Dr Daly has a strong interest in Spanish culture. Classroom and language laboratory work is enhanced through arts events held in Spanish. Students at Wollongong have reacted enthusiastically, with three-quarters of first-year students of Spanish continuing into second year. It shows, as always, the importance of engaging teaching.

Associate Professor Sankar Sinha is an award-winning teacher at the University of Tasmania, and an expert in the management of chronic wounds. He uses digital images to teach medical students, exploring complicated patient problems through online simulation before the class puts the lessons to work by meeting with patients firsthand.

In the Faculty of Health, Business and Science at the Northern Territory's Batchelor Institute of Indigenous Tertiary Education, Dr Kirstin Ross provides lectures and source material about public health then takes her students to the mines, tattoo parlours and hostels where public health issues must be addressed. Such teaching makes real the lessons of the classroom and provides an opportunity afterwards to reflect.

* * *

The campus is changing, but big questions about the purpose of teaching remain. Everyone might agree a university undergraduate degree should provide not just detailed information, built over at least three years of study, but the techniques by which new discoveries, new understandings, become possible.

Some argue for a further mission for universities, that of developing moral judgement in students. The timing is good — for young students in particular, university coincides with growing into adulthood. For some this proves a time of uncertainty and introspection, for others an opportunity for eager experiment. Campus is a place to work out who, and what, we want to be.

Universities are often reluctant to defend a moral role — who is to say which set of values should prevail? Public universities are secular and non-partisan, welcoming all creeds and none.

Yet written into the fabric of the institution are core beliefs about the importance of truth, knowledge and social justice. This means scholarly inquiry must be open and critical. As the Murray Report concluded in 1958, 'No nation ... wishes to make itself prone to self-delusion ... and a good university is the best guarantee ... that somebody, whatever the circumstances, will continue to seek the truth and make it known'.

There are values implicit in university mottos, in statements of graduate attributes, printed on the banners to fly on Open Days. In recent times the Australian Catholic University and Macquarie University, among others, have decided to make these values more visible, as they explore the moral dimension of higher education.

The Australian Catholic University (ACU) has created a Flagship for Creative and Authentic Leadership, designed to encourage moral and ethical guidance. ACU is writing core curriculum to reflect its Catholic mission and identity.

Steven Schwartz, Vice-Chancellor at Macquarie, champions teaching to build character through investigation of moral values. He argues that universities should do more than train people for the workforce and make their countries richer. People need jobs and students understandably worry about their careers, but Professor Schwartz suggests that to be successful — in a profession, in life — students need also to learn how to think, how to make decisions in difficult circumstances, how to be wise before and during the event. They need, in short, what Aristotle called 'practical wisdom'.

Macquarie has reshaped teaching so all students, whatever their major, are challenged to think about, and apply, moral and ethical decision-making.

University education, then, is about developing and broadening our capabilities as people, while training students to take on some of the most responsible roles in our society.

It is an impressive calling for academics. When Sir Thomas More suggests Richard Rich become a teacher in the play *A Man For All Seasons*, Rich is horrified. Even if I proved a great teacher, he asks, 'who would know it?'

'You, your pupils, your friends, God,' replies More. 'Not a bad public, that ...'

The great academic teachers are those who convey the excitement of their subject, their sense of what we know and what remains to be discovered.

For me, as an eighteen-year-old, it was hearing Elaine Thompson, Conal Condren and Donald Horne make vivid sense of politics for a large first-year class at the University of New South Wales. Through two semesters the teaching team weaved together three themes — the first, an analysis of how Australian political institutions work; the second, a broader examination of social trends in our nation; and the final theme, an introduction to political theory. The design was not always obvious to us students, yet at the end of our year we could see how the conversation between ideas, social forces and institutions maps the terrain for political life.

At the same time, a friend on campus was learning biological systems. His description of how one lecturer explained osmosis — by crawling around a half-open door into the lecture theatre, saying, 'Now I'm a water molecule permeating a membrane, moving from a small space to a larger one' — remains vivid decades later.

In a recent book about the Athenian navy, an American scholar recalls a vocation for ancient history that began with his very first lecture at Yale, when the professor 'marshalled the front row of students into an improvised phalanx of Greek warriors, with notebooks for shields and pens for spears, to demonstrate military manoeuvres'.

We recall always the inspired lecturer, their passion for their discipline, their sense of urgency about why this field of knowledge matters. It is the great teachers who bring alive the world of scholarship and research, in a university as nowhere else.

Whatever the subject matter, therefore, a university

education is more than technical training. The teaching must encompass reasoning, theory, method and ethics. A good measure of success is whether students acquire the ability to ask difficult questions, propose plausible answers, and test those hypotheses with evidence.

At the Australian National University, economist Martin Richardson uses a two-hour class to divide students into a simulation with five firms operating in different markets. Over seven or eight rounds of the game, teams watch competitors and learn from their strategies. If all goes well, the students see that however elegant the standard solutions of economics, in practice the business of price and quantity setting is pretty messy. And yet, they find, solutions do converge where we might expect, even when information is pretty limited.

Such lessons persist long after leaving campus. A graduate is trained to apply existing knowledge to new circumstances, to recognise that a line of thinking developed to solve one problem may work elsewhere.

At Open Day at the University of Technology, Sydney, engineering students demonstrate electric wheelchairs that can be steered by brain patterns. Designed originally as a vehicle to operate remotely in hostile environments, it did not take long for a student to grasp the vehicle's potential to help the disabled.

A university education is more than skills, more than a job qualification. It is an invitation to marvel at the world, to analyse and understand, and to act on the knowledge so acquired.

* * *

Can we put a value on good education, given that the personal and community returns seem hard to measure?

Jacob Mincer and Gary Becker — who won the 1992 Nobel Prize in Economics in part for work on education — have developed formal theories of 'human capital'. These seek to understand people as a factor of production.

Their pioneering work, and the many studies since, emphasise that training and education create a resource that has economic benefit. Human capital is an investment with measurable returns. A human-capital approach recognises that human knowledge and skills, as much as capital and machinery, contribute to prosperity.

This insight has become a key political defence for spending on universities — how can Australia develop a smart economy without well-educated people? Yet human capital can seem an unduly narrow prism through which to view education. Much that education offers speaks to other parts of our experience, interests beyond the economic. Most writing on higher education prefers broader measures of value, including the personal benefits of time at university.

As legal scholar Martha Nussbaum argues in *Not for Profit: Why democracy needs the humanities*, universities create citizens of the world. They prepare people to make a lifelong contribution. It is no coincidence the vast majority of our political, cultural and business leaders — in vocations that do not require a formal qualification — are nonetheless university graduates.

But then, what vice-chancellor would argue otherwise?

* * *

Learning and teaching matter — for our students and, argue the economists, for our nation. So it matters they are done well.

As the Australian university system has expanded, many worry about deteriorating standards of teaching. It is an understandable concern — since 1990, average class sizes have nearly doubled. The expansion of international education has created classrooms that are diverse but can also, at times, prove culturally and linguistically challenging.

Yet the evidence suggests an interesting outcome. Recent decades have been a time of measurement — indeed we have never before collected so much data on teaching performance and outcomes.

Every course, every semester, in every university, is evaluated by students. There are national data available to record student satisfaction and graduate outcomes. Academic boards ask pointed questions about courses and teachers with poor appraisal results. Classroom training is usually mandatory for new academic staff, while mentoring, feedback and structured reflection on teaching practices have become standard.

It is a testament to Australia's 43,000 academics that despite rising class sizes, measures show a steady improvement in student evaluation of the quality of their course and a marked increase on the good-teaching scale.

Thanks to this endless accounting, we know Australian institutions offer quality. But every student is different. Some prefer the personal contact of a small campus, and the chance to be part of a learning community. The colleges of the University of New England in Armidale have long provided a welcome destination for such students.

Others crave the excitement of large metropolitan institutions or the accessibility of nearby suburban campuses. Some students wish to move quickly through their degree, and value the annual three-semester models offered by Deakin and Bond universities. Others plan to study part-time over many years and look for institutions such as the Queensland University of Technology with a long tradition of evening classes and graduate study.

Such diversity allows students to choose the institution that works best for them. This means options about subjects, location, timing, classroom and online experience, breadth and, for private offerings, cost. Such specialisation helps the system speak to the widest array of students. There should not be one model of a university, but many. Institutions must be human-shaped, as varied as the communities and people they serve.

So Open Day is a presentation of difference, an advertisement for choice. It is the republic on display.

Visit Open Day next year and there, once more, will be those same academics standing alongside their professional staff colleagues. They turn up every August because they are loyal, because they care. Teaching may be a job, but it is also a joy. People work in universities not for the money, which is modest, nor the public acclaim, which is elusive. They come to work every day — many long after their formal retirement — because they love the chance to work with young people, to share with them the excitement of learning, to experience again the practical chemistry of teaching.

Open Day is but a glimpse of the university within, the republic of learning that is every campus.

Three
Research! A Mere Excuse for Idleness

University research takes a pressing problem and explores it from every angle. Specialists drawn from many fields and institutions race to understand the puzzle. As philosopher Michael Oakeshott said about universities in general, research is a 'conversation that does not need a chairman, it has no predetermined course ... and we do not judge its excellence by its conclusion ...'

For research has no conclusion, always just the next puzzle to explain.

Take disease. When modern humans left Africa more than 60,000 years ago, they carried not just cultures and languages that would spread across the planet, but less welcome passengers such as malaria.

Its effects have been felt ever since.

For most of human history the nature and causes of malaria

were not understood. Then, in 1902, the Nobel Prize in Medicine was awarded to Sir Ronald Ross, a British army surgeon working in India, who proved the malaria parasite is transmitted by mosquitoes.

His Nobel citation proclaimed that he had 'laid the foundation for successful research on this disease and methods of combating it'. Yet victory over the disease has been elusive. More than a century later, malaria still afflicts a significant proportion of humanity.

It is true malaria is all but eliminated from the developed world. Countries such as Australia record only a small number of cases — the result of travellers returning from affected areas. Yet in the developing world some 3.3 billion people remain at risk, half the world's population. Malaria has become a disease of the poor.

The research effort to address malaria is diverse and global. It engages social science experts in demographics, epidemiology, history and conflict, who work alongside geneticists, biologists, immunologists and an array of specialist medical researchers.

For malaria has proved a problem more complex than originally imagined. It has called into being a worldwide research effort — a grand endeavour beyond institutional boundaries or national borders, a manifestation of the republic of learning in which knowledge is shared and developed by communities of scholars. The endeavour to find a vaccine or long-term cure is the republic of learning at its best.

It suggests the character of contemporary research — driven by problems but operating without central coordination, a network of researchers who know each other's work through rapid publication, a virtual community that absorbs new developments quickly and incorporates them into a shared base of knowledge.

It is an approach that can produce remarkable results. Deadly diseases have been understood and eliminated already. Take smallpox. For perhaps 3000 years, smallpox killed up to one in three people infected by the virus. Those who survived carried scars for life, and many were afflicted with blindness. At the close of the eighteenth century, Edward Jenner tested his theory that milkmaids avoided smallpox by being infected with the less extreme cowpox. Over time this led to the development of a smallpox vaccination.

Although successful in 1796, it was not until 1967 that planning and technology could support a global eradication campaign on smallpox, which still threatened 60 per cent of the world's population. This World Health Organisation program proved astonishingly successful, drawing in large part on the research of Frank Fenner, an Australian expert in virology at the Australian National University. Within a decade the last naturally occurring case of smallpox was confined to Somalia. No further cases have been identified outside the laboratory anywhere on the planet during the past thirty years.

Similar hopes for eliminating malaria have been frustrated, despite an international effort and philanthropic support from the Gates Foundation. Malaria is a debilitating, and often fatal, disease. It is rife in sub-Saharan Africa, but is also a major cause of illness in the Asia-Pacific region. Society does poorly where malaria does well. It is hard to break the cycle of poverty when sickness prevails.

As Ronald Ross established, malaria is an infection of the blood, transmitted through a parasite of the mosquito. To reproduce, the female mosquito requires blood. If a person bitten is already infected with malaria, the parasite is taken in with the blood and begins the next stage of its life cycle. This only occurs in a warm climate — at less than 18°C transmission is unlikely. Malaria is therefore a disease of the tropical zone — at least for the moment, given the potential for shifts in climate and population.

Transmission begins when the mosquito takes a subsequent meal, allowing the parasite to transfer to a second person. Once the malaria parasite enters the blood stream, it finds and invades a red blood cell. The process only takes thirty seconds.

The parasite transforms the surface of the human red blood cell, making it sticky and able to attach to the wall of a blood vessel. Surface changes mean the infected cell will not be detected and destroyed by the immune system. The parasite then reproduces at an astonishing rate in this protected environment. As they reproduce and multiply, the parasites release toxins that cause fever. Some ten days after the mosquito bite the first symptoms emerge, usually headache and vomiting. As the disease progresses, symptoms become more severe.

Those infected with malaria risk major damage when the parasites attack the brain, the lungs and, in the case of pregnant women, the placenta. Anaemia is common, as red blood cells are destroyed and cannot be replaced. Respiratory distress occurs as the infection makes the blood more acidic, particularly in small children. Cerebral malaria occurs when infected cells stick to blood vessels in the brain. The patient becomes confused, suffers convulsions and falls into coma. Mortality is high, even where medical services are good.

The World Health Organisation reported over 247 million cases of malaria — and almost a million deaths — in 2008 alone. Most occur in Africa, where malaria contributes to around 20 per cent of all childhood deaths. Fatalities are lower in Asia, but malaria continues to claim lives and health in many parts of our region, including Papua New Guinea.

It is unlikely there will be a single solution to malaria. There appears to be no straight line from question to answer, only a slow realisation of how intricate nature can be, and the difficulties of preventing a disease that has spent tens of thousands of years adapting to humans.

The fight against malaria is therefore a classic research problem, requiring the combined intellect of public health professionals, social and biological scientists.

There are practical measures — education about risk, draining swamplands and other breeding grounds for mosquitoes, and supplying insect screen doors, windows and mosquito nets. Epidemiologists have identified the range of the disease and patterns of infection. Public health research encourages risk identification and prevention.

While no effective vaccination is available, pharmacologists have identified some compounds that inhibit or slow infection. Quinine was known from the seventeenth century, while today

Artemisinin is one of the most effective anti-malarial drugs, drawing on traditional Chinese medicine.

Because the malaria parasite quickly develops resistance to individual drugs, combination therapies are advocated. Even these are unlikely to remain effective, and in the longer term new approaches are required.

Eliminating swamps, use of insecticides, school education programs and the building of complex irrigation and dam systems eradicated malaria in Italy — a goal that took almost 100 years to achieve. This concerted government effort is not a viable strategy in much of Africa and Asia. For the moment, while the research is pursued across the world, the Roll Back Malaria Partnership advocates a combination of new anti-malaria drugs, pesticides, vaccination research, the distribution of insecticide-treated bed netting and landscape management.

As Dr Halima Mwenesi, an expert in public health and policy working in South Africa, observed:

> … insights from anthropology; sociology; demography and geography; health economics and policy; social psychology; epidemiology; and behaviour-change communication have permeated all areas of our response to malaria. We now know how humans respond to malaria and this knowledge has enabled us to build fairly strong multidisciplinary malaria prevention, management and control programs.

Mwenesi observed that, until recently, a contribution from the social sciences seemed an afterthought to scientific work on malaria. It has taken bitter experience to realise the solution will not be found in biochemistry alone. While we wait for a cure, malaria continues to kill millions.

Because human beings are integral to the life cycle of the parasite, our activities and responses to the disease matter. Understanding human behaviour is the province of the humanities and social sciences. Hence recent decades have seen a significant contribution to fighting malaria from experts who study the range, history and distribution of people in infected areas, their religious beliefs and gender roles, patterns of trade, ceremony and interaction, local understandings of illness, and the most effective ways to achieve behavioural change.

Infected women and children usually sicken and die in their homes. How to alert medical services to their illness? How to arrange diagnosis in communities without doctors, or administer precise dosages when people lack familiarity with western medicine?

Social science has encouraged experiment and monitoring. In some communities, for example, shopkeepers can be trained to diagnose and treat malaria-like illness. They are more likely to have routine contact with patients and are trusted community members.

Malaria intervention at the local level depends on understanding the consequences of gender and poverty, and cultural norms about compliance. By researching how people live and move, public health officials are able to predict the spread of the disease and evaluate the effectiveness of measures to contain the sickness.

It is one thing to develop effective anti-malaria strategies in the laboratory, another entirely to predict how the campaign will be accepted by those who must adopt its measures.

* * *

Australia has long made a strong contribution to this global effort. The identification of malaria in northern Australia led to the establishment of the Institute of Tropical Medicine in Townsville in 1910, followed by the School of Public Health and Tropical Medicine at the University of Sydney in 1930.

During the Second World War, malaria posed a significant threat to Australian troops. Physician Neil Fairley left the London School of Hygiene and Tropical Medicine to work with Australian soldiers as they fought in malaria-infected theatres. His field observations helped increase understanding of the disease and promote use of the few available anti-malaria drugs.

In the following decades, research leaders such as Graham Mitchell and Sir Gus Nossal encouraged scientists to apply recent advances in biomedical research to address infectious diseases of global significance. The establishment of a dedicated malaria group at the Walter and Eliza Hall Institute of Medical Research in Melbourne signalled a strong commitment to the field — and recognition that complex problems require large teams, long timeframes and sustained funding.

There have been moments of great hope. In the 1980s, Dr David Kemp, Robin Anders and their teams working at the

Walter and Eliza Hall Institute created a genetically engineered prototype vaccine. A partnership with the Queensland Institute of Medical Research, CSL, Biotechnology Australia, and the Papua New Guinea Institute of Medical Research supported vaccine trials.

Meanwhile, also at the Walter and Eliza Hall Institute, Professor Alan Cowman used molecular biology techniques to understand drug resistance. He developed a technique for adding and removing parasite genes, which offered the prospect of reducing the danger from the parasite, while stimulating an immune response if given to humans.

Today Dr Krystal Evans continues that research, seeking a gene-based solution to malaria. She and her colleagues pursue the vision of a 'live, genetically modified, vaccine against *Plasmodium falciparum*, the parasite that causes the form of malaria most deadly to humans'.

Close by, at La Trobe University, biochemist Professor Leann Tilley collaborates with physicists to develop sharper images of the malarial parasite at work within individual cells.

Two thousand kilometres north, at the Queensland Institute of Medical Research in Brisbane, Dr Tim Hurst works on controlling mosquitoes at the household level, with the goal of reducing the spread of diseases.

Not far away at the School of Population Health within the University of Queensland, Professor Maxine Whittaker is collaborating on regional responses through the Asia Pacific Malaria Elimination Network.

At the Research School of Biology at the ANU in Canberra,

Dr Kiaran Kirk and Dr Rowena Martin, a recent recipient of a Eureka Prize for Early Career Research, seek ways to combat malaria drug resistance.

In Perth, postgraduate physicist Stephan Karl at the University of Western Australia, continues his award-winning work on the changing magnetic properties of malaria-infected cells; while in Hobart, Professor Simon Foote leads a team at the Menzies Research Institute Tasmania investigating different host responses to infection.

As the Hobart team observes, though the malaria parasite infects many infants, only some succumb to the disease. If they can understand the reasons for these differences, it may be possible to develop new anti-malaria therapies, particularly for children.

At the University of Newcastle, Dr Janet Dzator with the Faculty of Business and Law has investigated links between health and economic development, with an emphasis on malaria control programs in Africa.

In Darwin, the Menzies School of Health Research works to understand better the impact of *P. vivax*, the form of malaria prominent in the Asia-Pacific region.

* * *

This brief survey barely sketches the depth and quality of malaria research across Australia. Just one problem among many, the quest to end malaria shows that large problems require complex answers, significant time and often substantial resources. The contemporary research model is cross-disciplinary, involving many institutions, international partnerships and international funding.

In research, the republic of learning extends beyond universities to embrace institutes, hospitals, think tanks, government departments, pharmaceutical companies, start-ups and not-for-profits. All share a passion for understanding the fundamentals of our world and ourselves.

These many different institutions must compete for a limited pool of research funding and even more limited public interest. Yet, from disease control to economic theory, the work done by our researchers can be life-changing.

Research can be personally inspiring, but challenging all the same. Dr Krystal Evans explains:

There is something about the thrill of the chase when you are seeking the answers to your questions that I find extremely rewarding. On a day-to-day level, research can be very repetitive; incredibly precise and exacting. But I've been to malaria-endemic countries, I've seen malaria in action, not just down a microscope, and so that keeps me going.

* * *

Research is not an ancient function of Australian universities. For the first century of tertiary education in Australia, the purpose of a university was teaching. Following British tradition, universities imparted knowledge and good character to their students. In *The Idea of a University*, written in 1852,

John Henry Newman saw cultivation of the intellect through teaching universal knowledge as the sole purpose of a university. There could be no place for research. Scientific and philosophical discovery were not appropriate for an institution focused on students. For Newman, scholars engaged in teaching were too busy to do research, while those engaged in research were much too preoccupied for teaching.

It was a tradition that could see classicist Benjamin Jowett, Master of Balliol College at Oxford, growl: 'Research! A mere excuse for idleness; it has never achieved, and will never achieve any results of the slightest value.'

Yet outside Britain, very different understandings of the university had emerged. Wilhelm von Humboldt established the idea of a research–teaching nexus in Berlin in 1810. This German research tradition in higher education was carried to the United States, first to east-coast private universities, and soon after to the land-grant public universities established from 1862. These proved important first in agricultural, and then in scientific and engineering research, helping America become the world's industrial centre.

The idea that university teaching should be animated by research, and indeed that a university might play an important role in technological development, was not well received in Australia. Early attempts to hire academics with a research interest proved controversial. The duty of a professor, said one council member at the University of Melbourne in 1878, is to 'impart, not invent'.

It would take decades before universities acquired the people, the facilities — and the confidence — to make research core to their vision. The first Australian doctoral student did not graduate until 1948. In that same decade the Australian National University and the University of New South Wales were established, both with charters to contribute to national progress through fundamental research.

By the time Australian universities embraced research as a central function, they no longer had the field to themselves. In 1926 the Australian Government turned an existing advisory body into the Council for Scientific and Industrial Research, an organisation that in 1949 was renamed, and flourishes still, as the CSIRO (Commonwealth Scientific and Industrial Research Organisation). From an initial focus on primary and secondary industries — farming, mining and manufacture — the CSIRO has become 'Australia's national science agency and one of the largest and most diverse research agencies in the world'.

The research space was filled also with the first medical research institutes, often with a focus on a particular disease or condition. Many of Australia's hospitals undertake world-leading research, often with crucial links to patient care and the coordination of clinical trials.

In this small world, a handful of medical researchers have become national heroes, and rightly so. Peter Doherty is celebrated for his joint discovery of how the immune system recognises virus-infected cells; Barry Marshall and Robin Warren for proving that spiral bacteria cause stomach ulcers; Ian Frazer for finding a vaccine for the papilloma virus that causes cervical cancer; and Elizabeth Blackburn for explaining the implications for health and aging of telomeres, the caps that protect chromosomes.

They are matched by public intellectuals from the humanities and social sciences, who speak about our lives together. Historians and anthropologists, demographers and English-literature specialists all help us grasp who and what we are.

As the fight against malaria shows, research is a continuum — pure and applied, basic and practical, across fields and domains, hard to predict or direct. What appears obtuse at one time can become central; knowledge is not divisible, but always connected.

Just as we need different sorts of universities to offer distinct visions of education, so research problems require competing teams and diverse groupings of academic disciplines. As with malaria, what today seems a scientific problem, to be addressed by unlocking some subtle mechanism of nature, may tomorrow be understood as primarily about human behaviour, best approached by designing new social, cultural or economic institutions.

* * *

What, then, enables the best research?

Well, money helps. Australia has a modest record when it comes to research investment, spending a similar ratio of gross domestic product as Canada and Great Britain but far less than the United States, Japan or South Korea. Australian research agencies cannot afford to fund fully those projects they support — and with limited resources, often only one in five grant applications is successful.

But good research requires more than cash. It needs a supportive environment, which means recognising that economic returns may be distant, even impossible. It requires time and encouragement, support to explore the intriguing, knowing the results may prove inconsequential.

Research needs the best and most committed minds. It demands patience, integrity, a willingness to take risks, and a high tolerance for failure, since much will not work, or not produce the hoped-for results. In a world of blind alleys, the research process demands we push towards acquiring new knowledge in spite of inevitable disappointments along the journey.

Given this essential character of research, there is no point prescribing expected outcomes. Discovery cannot be planned or mandated. Researchers begin with a goal in mind, but the more complex the problem, the less certain the path. Hence the importance of multiple teams, competing approaches, different theories about an issue. 'The best way to have a good idea,' said twice Nobel Prize-winning chemist Linus Pauling, 'is to have a lot of ideas.' The research community works best when many paths are explored simultaneously.

Instant publication via the web ensures knowledge is spread quickly, and insights from one approach quickly inform teams elsewhere. Through the logic of testing hypotheses — what Karl Popper described as making 'our successive mistakes as quickly as possible' — knowledge advances.

There are heartbreaks along the way, and the path can be long. In the 1970s a breakthrough seemed imminent when researchers proved able to cultivate malaria in a laboratory.

Similar successes for polio led to widely used live vaccines. These trigger an immune response and the body learns how to defeat any future infection. Sadly the technique did not work for malaria.

Attention then switched to genetic solutions, made possible by the advances in cultivating malaria in the lab. Again, the logic seemed promising. Malaria produces proteins that stimulate the immune system. Biologists learned to isolate the genes that make these proteins and copy them into living organisms such as *e. coli* capable of producing the protein in vast quantities. When injected with the protein, our bodies should produce the necessary immune response to fight malaria.

Yet progress has been disappointing. It proved difficult to find the right proteins. Variation means it has been challenging to trigger an immune response, just as high variability in the common cold virus leaves us susceptible even though we have been infected many times before. Three decades of gene-based research have produced only a few prototype vaccines, with only one at the Phase 3 trial stage.

So attention has returned to infection prevention, and to live vaccines for the mosquito stage of malaria. Researchers now study how the human body responds to the entire malaria organism. A line of research largely abandoned thirty years ago has renewed hope of an effective response.

This is how research proceeds — building on previous knowledge, trying and failing, pursuing many options in the hope one will provide the next step forward.

Public investment in such research produces two key benefits for society.

Benefits:

The first is all around us — the numerous ways our lives are made better. Improvements to health science have produced an almost three-fold improvement in life expectancy for the developed world, and hope for similar outcomes for all humanity. Research can cure a disease, provide the gift of hearing, explain how to improve outcomes in primary classrooms, and help us to understand the language, culture and philosophy of our neighbours and ourselves.

Rolling back malaria is not just about developing new and better medicines. By freeing people from a debilitating disease we provide them with a chance to realise their capability, to make their contribution, to do more than worry about the survival of their children.

The second benefit is the opportunity opened up for the human race. At its most impressive, research speaks truth to power, embodying the Enlightenment ideal of using evidence to interrogate the world.

In this sense, research is a public good — a contribution to humanity that cannot be valued with conventional measures, yet proves essential for a fragile planet.

Research confronts us with inconvenient truths, unwelcome insights. We now debate climate change because accumulated research indicates this is a major issue. Some argue with the evidence, as they should. But the sheer weight of evidence makes the risks hard to ignore. We must hope research findings will influence policy choices. Knowledge can liberate, motivating us to tackle the problems of the world.

* * *

Each university campus contains a microcosm of the republic of learning. Within its walls are experts in political science, architecture, physics, demography, Indigenous studies, education, genetics, economics and classics. Researchers interact. Unexpected projects and alliances form. As problems change, as new ideas emerge, so do the conversations across campus. New knowledge is generated between, as well as within, buildings.

Because universities endure, their research effort is continuous and long-lived. Abandoned threads can be revived, new disciplines embraced. The research team can be reconfigured to suit the problem. Knowledge may be codified in journal articles and monographs, but it is carried forward by a living community, an endless transmission from teacher to student, from peer to peer, from professor to the newest research associate. The tradition of graduate research training means the generations overlap continuously, each learning from the other.

Every malaria researcher might hope to solve the problem, but it is more likely the students they train who will prevail.

Research reflects, and expresses, the spirit of the university and the wider republic of learning at its most inspirational. No mere excuse for idleness, research is the way we investigate — and change — our world.

Four
Becoming a Citizen

Our theme is the republic of learning — the world of higher education inspired by the humanist scholars of the Renaissance. In this chapter I want to ask some awkward questions: How democratic is our republic? Who gets to be a citizen? And how do we ensure universities serve individuals and communities across this nation?

Today we equate republicanism with democracy. It was not always so. For most of human history, republicanism was associated with a virtuous elite. This is no longer acceptable. Equality of opportunity has become the rule. People expect university entry to be based strictly on the principle of merit. Elitism — at least elitism based on something other than intellectual ability — is untenable.

If Australia is to be a meritocracy, drawing in students from all walks of life is essential.

So where do we begin this quest for a democratic republic of learning? At the beginning … with school.

* * *

Sean and Adam Tunks are primary school students at Sanctuary Point Public School, about 25 kilometres south of Nowra on the New South Wales south coast. Their mother teaches at the school, and the family are active in the nearby St Georges Basin community. It is a beautiful area, close to beaches, and quiet, except in summer when tourists arrive in their thousands.

The Tunks family illustrates how education has changed over several generations. For while Sean and Adam's parents, grandparents and great-grandparents would recognise the familiar literacy and numeracy lessons of primary school, their opportunities and expectations were very different.

For Sean and Adam's great-grandfather Edward, education ended early. Edward finished school at sixteen and became a drover, before labouring on construction of the Burrinjuck Dam. He spent time in the army and worked in a lino factory. Like the men of his generation, Edward could move between jobs, learning skills at work, with little formal instruction. Going to university was rare in Edward's generation, open to perhaps one in twenty young Australians.

Edward's son Harry, Sean and Adam's grandfather, left school in the early 1950s with his intermediate certificate, to become a builder. Times were changing, with a growing emphasis on organised education. Harry's training as a builder involved an apprenticeship and study at Granville Technical College. Harry subsequently worked as a licensed builder, assisting construction of the 2000 Sydney Olympics Cauldron.

Most of Harry's generation of Australians did not seek post-school education. Many careers were open to those with no formal qualifications, while some professions were still entered via admissions tests rather than universities. Dentistry, for example, was an apprenticeship in New South Wales until the 1930s. University study was not compulsory for admission to legal practice until the mid 1960s. Accounting, nursing and journalism did not require tertiary-level study until recently.

Still, while Harry was young, the university sector began to expand. From just 30,000 students across all of Australia in the 1950s, university enrolments reached 100,000 by the middle of the 1960s. Only then did specialised intakes and strict cut-off scores appear. Previously, few faculties imposed quotas. Once accepted to university, students could choose law or medicine, arts or engineering.

For Harry's generation, further education was principally men's business. The gender roles of their times saw men as breadwinners. Only single women would need to keep themselves afloat with a job. So men were more likely than women to stay at school beyond the compulsory years, and more likely to complete a post-school qualification.

Women not only had less access to education, but many were compelled to leave the workforce when they marrried, a rule still operating in the Australian Public Service in 1966. Such restrictions discouraged women from acquiring professional qualifications or pursuing a career. (Incidentally, the man who recommended abolition of the marriage bar was Sir Richard Boyer, in whose memory this lecture series is named.)

Some women refused to be deterred, but on average university classes for this generation were mostly male. Until the early 1970s, two-thirds of university students were men. And universities tended to welcome the middle class. Though teaching scholarships were available to some, for many young people fees stood in the way of higher education.

Harry's daughter Gemma was born into a very different world. During the 1970s and 1980s the labour market for teenage school leavers deteriorated sharply. Gemma's mother worked to help support her four children, while women of Gemma's generation expected to study and choose professional careers.

In 1994 Gemma enrolled at the then Nepean campus of the University of Western Sydney (UWS), studying a Bachelor of Teaching (Primary). The University of Western Sydney was then a very new university, recently formed by amalgamating two former colleges of advanced education with an agricultural college. Committed to serving the greater west of Sydney, a region with historically low participation in higher education, UWS is rightly proud of the opportunities it provides. Higher education can transform lives and communities.

Like a majority of UWS students, Gemma was the first in her family to go to university. She faced a long commute, and eventually moved in with her sister, who lived closer to campus. During her studies, Gemma undertook four teaching placements at local schools. Her course included foundation disciplines such as maths and English, history, the creative arts and Australian studies.

Gemma graduated at the end of 1996 and accepted a job at Busby West Primary School.

Later she returned to UWS part-time to complete a further degree. When her family left the western suburbs of Sydney for St Georges Basin in 2005, Gemma joined Sanctuary Point Primary School as a temporary teacher.

Gemma's generation is the first in which girls were as likely as boys to complete Year 12. By the 1980s two out of every three teenagers completed high school, and this trend fuelled expectations of a place on campus.

The result was an unprecedented expansion of university places. Australian universities added a quarter of a million students between 1987 and 1997. About one in four of this generation ended up with a university qualification.

That year, 1987, was a turning point in Australian education: the first year female students outnumbered men on campus, a pattern that continues. Gemma was part of that new majority, studying for a profession that now demands a university qualification.

On current federal government projections, her sons will likely be among the 40 per cent of young Australians who will study at university. Even more will seek a TAFE or vocational qualification.

Right now, at ages eight and nine, Sean and Adam are thinking of careers in the military — just one of many organisations in which further education is now mandatory. Officers receive a university degree at the Australian Defence Force Academy, part of the University of New South Wales. Modern weaponry requires high-level technical skills, along with the courage and endurance always expected of the military.

We cannot say with certainty how much education Sean, Adam and their generation will need to prosper as adults. But during the decades from Edward and Harry to Gemma, from the post-war era to today, formal education has become part of family expectations. Edward left school early, like most of his contemporaries. His son studied for a TAFE qualification, while his granddaughter would see a bachelors degree as essential. No doubt Gemma's aspirations for Sean and Adam include an important role for further education.

The Tunks family trace a broader Australian social change. In just three generations, higher education has moved from the margins of society to its mainstream. Men and women now participate on equal terms. If the government's targets are met — and few doubt the acceleration of higher education will continue — today's primary school students are eight times as likely to go to university as their great-grandparents.

The republic of learning, once the preserve of an elite, is now on the road to democracy.

* * *

This new world of education and work offers exciting opportunities. There are more interesting and well-paid jobs than ever before. For those with professional qualifications, a global labour market offers work in Shanghai, London or New York.

Though graduates start work later in life, they earn significantly more over their lifetime. An education is an investment that keeps on returning.

Yet a world of credentials also creates new risks. For younger adults today, the lack of a university or higher-level vocational qualification doubles their chance of unemployment.

Less education is statistically linked to lower income, a higher chance of poor physical or mental health, less involvement in community and civic life, and for men a lesser chance of getting and staying married. Missing out on education flows through to every part of life.

Education is part of what the economist and philosopher Amartya Sen calls 'capabilities'. The right collection of capabilities allow us lives we find meaningful, productive and rewarding — lives we have reason to value. A capability is more than a liberty, because we may lack the capacity to do things we are permitted. And it is not an outcome, because people use their capabilities in very different ways.

In this approach to social policy, the goal should be to ensure every person has a basket of capabilities — health, literacy and numeracy, sufficient income to meet basic needs, social skills and enough education to meet the demands of their times.

There is a collective dimension to this understanding. Along with individual capabilities, education brings benefits to a community. By every measure, from health outcomes to civic involvement, an educated community offers better outcomes for its members. Higher education helps develop community life and shared expertise. Such outcomes provide an argument for equity that goes well beyond the possibilities education opens for individuals.

Viewed through this frame, access to education is a moral question. Since education links to so many other aspects of life, when educational capabilities are not shared fairly in our community, prosperity and wellbeing will not be shared fairly either.

So how to guarantee that everyone has an opportunity to become a citizen in the republic of learning?

* * *

That question has dominated recent research on education outcomes. What explains differences in educational outcomes? What is the role of universities, and government, in ensuring access and equity of opportunity? In a public education system, regulated and substantially funded by government, the question of who participates should be a political issue.

Meeting the demand for education has been a major challenge for state and federal governments. School retention rates slowly increased through the 1960s and 1970s before soaring in the 1980s. TAFE enrolments also grew significantly, to reach around 1.7 million students a year. Domestic university enrolments now number around 800,000, with another 200,000 international students studying in Australia. While the wider population has less than tripled since the 1950s, the domestic university student population has increased twenty-six-fold.

Good policies have made this outcome possible. There has been a sustained push to increase the proportion of young people reaching Year 12. Flexible entry criteria have increased opportunities for further study for disadvantaged students, the mature-aged and those graduating from TAFE. There are more part-time study options available and there is access to income support through Youth Allowance and Austudy. There are more campuses, and an innovative student loans program, the Higher Education Contribution Scheme, allows students to postpone paying for their course until they earn decent wages.

Taken in aggregate, these policies have achieved a remarkable result: our school system provides a place to Year 12 for every Australian child, and most young adults can then secure a place at a university or TAFE to further their education.

There is no evidence that overt discrimination based on gender, ethnicity or other characteristics systemically excludes people from higher education.

Yet, despite this continued success in boosting overall enrolment numbers, a stubborn and unresolved problem remains: social background matters a great deal in how much education you receive. Your choice of parents and the community in which you live affect your basket of capabilities.

Parents differ in how much they value study, and how much they can support children's education. Many families live far from high-quality schools and access to a TAFE or university campus. For people in regional areas, and particularly Indigenous Australians in remote communities, further education options are often very limited.

The influence of family and place is complex, but some patterns are clear. If a parent holds a university degree, there is a 50 per cent chance their daughter or son will attend university soon after completing school.

Thereafter the odds fall sharply. For parents who finished their education at Year 12, the chances of their children getting to university halve to one in four. And for those who did not finish school, there is just a one in five chance of the next generation going to campus.

Parents who value education for themselves are likely to pass that attitude on to their children. University-educated parents can give their children advice and academic help, paying if necessary for tuition or private schooling. Children follow in their parents' footsteps. Advantage is passed down through generations — as is disadvantage.

Yet a parent's past is not a straitjacket from which children cannot escape. The history of migration to Australia makes this clear. Parents who missed out on higher education but come from communities that value learning, and create a home that supports study, will encourage their children to pursue further learning. Many Vietnamese families — like the family of Nam Le, author of the prize-winning fiction volume *The Boat* — arrived in Australia as refugees, their lives disrupted by war and persecution. Nam Le, three months old when his family reached Australia, says his parents arrived with nothing but the shorts and T-shirts they wore. Yet by working multiple jobs and encouraging their children to study, this refugee generation has given today's Australia some of its most outstanding achievers: like

Nam Le, himself a law graduate and today fiction editor of *Harvard Review.*

Such a trajectory is not unique. Young Australians of Vietnamese background, strongly encouraged by their parents, are much more likely than the broader population to attend university, and to excel.

There are many inspiring stories of individuals overcoming disadvantage to secure an education, and with it a better life. Even in our least affluent communities, 20 per cent of young Australians find their way to TAFE or university. But given the many advantages through life from education, any difference in access raises a pressing question of fairness. How do we close the gap in educational attainment?

* * *

Our national challenge is to ensure full admission to the republic of learning, and the capabilities that education helps provide, for every Australian.

The answer must begin in the early years. As recent research confirms, family life, child care and initial schooling all have a big effect on future development. The Nobel Prize-winning economist James Heckman has demonstrated that children who fall behind by age eight are unlikely ever to catch up.

Australian evidence supports this grim finding. One study of 10,000 children found that by age four or five there are clear socio-economic differences in learning. The most recent NAPLAN test results, reported on the *My School* website, show the influence of parental education by age eight. In writing and numeracy tests, children of parents with university qualifications are already well ahead of the average. By contrast, the children of parents who finished school in Year 11 are much less likely to meet the minimum standard.

These gaps in literacy and numeracy remain large at Year 9, when students are aged about fourteen.

Whether or not university is the aim, literacy and numeracy are essential skills for other learning. Weaknesses in the early years undermine capabilities and flow through to less education, lower incomes and difficulties in managing everyday tasks, such as understanding correspondence and instructions, following maps, reading timetables, calculating costs. An inability to help children with their homework reinforces inherited disadvantage.

Consistent with the research, federal and state governments are focusing on the beginning of a child's life. Improved neonatal care aims to reduce disadvantages that begin so early. Programs that teach parenting skills hope to improve outcomes for children. There is recognition of the need for greater investment in the quality and availability of early childhood education — but still much, much more to be done.

* * *

These initiatives will take a long time to flow through to university entry. The National Early Childhood Development Strategy is based on a vision for the year 2020. Children who receive its full benefits that year will be ready for university entry around 2038. We can't wait that long. So there must be an immediate focus on better schools and better pathways for those who have already left school.

Crucial to this national effort is the dedication of schoolteachers — teachers like Gemma Tunks, mother of Sean and Adam.

Our kindergarten teachers are often the first great formative influence beyond the family, and school our first experience of working with a group of strangers and living alongside difference. School gives us a glimpse of something bigger than ourselves and our immediate circle. It's an invitation to open the mind.

Schoolteachers are the quiet heroes in our communities, daily adding to the knowledge and social skills of young Australians. The educational transformation of Australia over recent generations is built on their work. The task now is to invest in teaching, taking our schools to the next level of skill and professionalism.

The people who teach the teachers — the education faculties around the nation — are thinking carefully about how to do so. The Melbourne Graduate School of Education, for example, has shifted professional training to graduate level, choosing graduates with strong undergraduate degrees in their respective fields and the maturity to know that school teaching is really their preferred career. A new curriculum with early immersion in classroom practice prepares the next generation of teachers.

Getting good people excited about providing education for the disadvantaged is the ambition of the Teach for Australia program. Teach for Australia takes talented graduates from all disciplines with leadership and communication skills, and gives them intense training while teaching in underprivileged schools for two years.

It is too early to test results from Teach for Australia against other forms of teacher training, but similar programs overseas are encouraging. This is one of the most exciting innovations in the teaching profession in recent years — the republic of learning sending out its brightest ambassadors to advocate the importance of education.

Such initiatives sit alongside the national curriculum, better identification of students and schools at risk through national testing, more information for parents, and more autonomy and accountability for school leaders. It is an agenda that puts students at the centre of the policy conversation.

* * *

To suggest that equality of opportunity must begin with preschool is not to let universities off the hook. Issues of fairness cannot be deferred a generation. A democratic republic of learning must look to the current enrolment and teaching practices of universities.

If we have a shared image of a university student, it is of a young person who recently completed Year 12 and went immediately to campus. This is misleading — most Australian university first-year students did not come straight from school. Universities draw on a wider constituency, with many students arriving with work experience and vocational qualifications.

But a challenge remains — how to encourage those now in school to go the next step, and those who left education some time ago to consider further study.

At the University of Ballarat, current undergraduates visit Year 10 classes in their old secondary colleges, to lift aspirations and offer practical advice about university life, from moving out of home to securing income support. The Year 10 students then spend a day on campus to get a feel for university life.

James Cook University (JCU) in northern Queensland recognises that many disadvantaged people could benefit from university education. This is particularly true of Indigenous people, who have much lower school completion rates than the rest of the community, and remain the group of Australians most seriously under-represented on campus. JCU offers a six-month tertiary access course, primarily designed for Indigenous students, so people who did not finish school can prepare for university-level study.

For many adult students, the path to university can be through a TAFE course. Australia's five 'dual sector' universities — institutions that offer both higher education and TAFE courses — are skilled at encouraging progression. Former TAFE students make up 20 per cent or more of the undergraduate intake. They may follow the example of Cassandra Fahey, who began from modest origins.

'I never went to private schools,' she told one interviewer. 'My dad went to Broady High and my mum went to school in Swan Hill and left when she was thirteen.' Fahey found her way to TAFE studies in art and design at the Box Hill Institute

up to 19 dual sector?

and then moved to an architectural degree at RMIT University. A talented and imaginative student, she was accepting commissions before completing her studies, and is now among the most successful of her generation of architects.

Cassandra Fahey is humble about her achievement. 'We're lucky in this country,' she notes. 'You're taken on face value and if you do good things, that's fine.' She is now studying for a masters degree in architecture.

Yet overall data suggest public universities have not done enough to extend higher learning to disadvantaged Australians.

Some take a tough-minded position on this failing, arguing that public universities have used their near-monopoly on government supported places to shape the higher education system in their own interests. Academic excellence is a virtue for the modern university, with its emphasis on original research and informed scholarship. But does it necessarily serve the interests of students or promote wider access to higher education?

Any system based on rewarding academic achievement will favour those whose parents hold university degrees or have other social advantages. At school, the preoccupation in Years 11 and 12 with achieving university admission invites a focus on the most academically able.

Ranking applicants by prior academic achievement is not the only possible system, but it reflects the interests and priorities of universities. High-achieving students enhance university prestige. They are often well prepared to be self-directed learners, and so easier to teach. And they are more likely to become researchers and the next generation of scholars, turning the academic cycle.

Yet if we view universities as gatekeepers to the professions, it is not so obvious that prior academic achievement is the best sorting device. Employers seek a much wider range of skills and attributes in their staff than just academic results. By filtering access to the professions through narrow tests of academic ability, many people never get to show what they can offer.

Greater flexibility in selection criteria — above a minimum necessary for admission — is part of the answer. Some universities already include aptitude tests and personal statements in deciding admission. Others give priority to applicants from disadvantaged backgrounds. Universities ask teachers from schools in challenging areas to nominate talented students who could do well in further study even if their final marks would not secure a place on campus.

Once students secure a place, it is not certain the organisation of university life will work in their interests. Though HECS removes up-front fees, the costs of living while at university can exclude families from regional Australia.

And there is no flexibility in the price of study. All Commonwealth-supported undergraduate places in a particular course cost the same, regardless of university. This limits choice, since public universities double as research institutions and so cluster at the expensive end of the spectrum.

There are arguments too about the structure of the academic year. Though the long summer break has distant origins in students going home to help with the harvest, it is now a student-free time so academics can work without interruption on their research. Put aside this delay, and the standard three-year undergraduate course could be completed in two years — something that would make university more accessible to workers and parents.

Of course, many students prefer the current system. They like studying in a research institution, in being close to people at the cutting edge of their field, and want to take time to absorb the lessons. They use the summer breaks to travel, broaden their reading, work to finance their study. For many students, university is a time of exploration before the rigours of adult life become too constraining, and summer the gift of what Michael Oakeshott called 'an interval' — an opportunity to 'put aside the hot allegiances of youth without the necessity of at once acquiring new loyalties to take their place'.

But in a more democratic republic of learning, there will be greater diversity of students. Some want time to broaden their intellectual horizons; others will seek quickly to build qualifications. People will start university at different stages of life, and expect institutions to accommodate their varied circumstances.

It is not clear the single model of an Australian public university is equipped to deal with this expanded spectrum of students. A wider range of institutions, each meeting the needs of different students, may be an important part of meeting our equity challenge. It is a theme for the final lecture of this series.

* * *

At Sanctuary Point Public School, students prepare for a future that will be as different as the world experienced successively

85

by Edward, Harry and Gemma. Their descendants, Sean and Adam, will not finish school until around 2020. Waiting for them should be the best possible universities, technical and further education institutions, offering a quality of education that will equip today's primary school students to work until 2065 or later.

It is important every child at Sanctuary Point — and everyone already beyond primary school years — has access to higher education. All Australians, whatever their means, should feel encouraged to participate. Only when citizenship is available to all who seek will we realise the potential of this republic of learning.

Five
Fired with Enthusiasm

The Griffith flag is deepest red
the memo from Karyn Brinkley said,
with corporate sign in glistening white
and branding icon in 12-point type.

> So raise the scarlet standard high
> and praise our university.
> Our trademark stands above the fray
> the red flag flies on open day.

In loco parentis *we proudly stand*
The red, the white, the black armband
The critics sneer we've lost our souls
but hey, we've met our marketing goals.

> *So raise the scarlet standard high*
> *and praise our university,*
> *Our trademark stands above the fray*
> *the red flag flies on open day.*

Welcome to the new university: a place where the old fights with the new.

Where scholars in medieval gowns sit incongruously beneath corporate-branding symbols.

Where Griffith University in south-east Queensland abandons its elaborate original coat of arms, with curlicues and rampant lions, for an open book on a bright red background.

Where customary pastimes such as democratic free speech and student protest jostle for attention with new business imperatives to promote, recruit and graduate.

And where to survive, universities must sell themselves — like never before.

* * *

Every republic must obtain the assent of the governed — and, inevitably, leave the governed just a little disappointed. Our 500-year-old republic of learning is no exception. Yet our universities have endured, retaining the symbols and forms of governance of centuries ago while adapting to very different circumstances.

It is a world in which university management is mocked with enthusiasm by people both sceptical of authority and deeply attached to their institution and its traditions.

The *Times Higher Education* journal — published in Britain

but widely read in Australian universities — devotes its back page to a newsletter conveying staff news from the fictional University of Poppleton. There are wonderful stock characters easily recognised by real-life citizens of universities — the corporate director of 'the ever-expanding HR department', the permanently absent vice-chancellor, the self-serving professor of media and cultural studies, always with a new research study of doubtful value requiring exotic travel. One regular character is a university official who glories in the title 'deputy director of logo development'.

University satire has a rich history. The tradition of students taking the micky out of teachers, comrades and the campus goes back a long way. It's a ritual that nurtures some of our nation's leading talent.

For example, in November 1941 a youthful Gough Whitlam appeared as Noel Coward in the St Paul's College revue at the University of Sydney. Biographer Jenny Hocking refers to a ten-minute monologue in which Whitlam impersonated the British actor and playwright farewelling the students after a tour of the university. It was a scene that allowed the future prime minister an early opportunity to showcase his acerbic wit 'to rapturous acclaim'.

Writes Hocking: 'No doubt concurring with Coward that "I love criticism just so long as it's unqualified praise", Gough sent a letter to his parents, enclosing a clipping extolling his remarkable impersonation.' The habits of a lifetime, it seems, can begin on campus.

The 'campus novel' has long found a place in Australia. Don Aitkin wrote *The Second Chair* at Macquarie University,

Ross Fitzgerald *Pushed From the Wings* at Griffith. Frank Moorhouse recalled interactions with academics in *Conference-ville*, while in *Tales of Mystery and Romance* he describes a good English tutorial as 'like intellectual nude wrestling'.

The late Laurie Clancy, who taught at La Trobe University, published a campus comedy titled *The Wildlife Reserve*. It includes a vice-chancellor who believes that to convince Canberra the institution is on the right track, a university administrator should promote the credo of amalgamation, privatisation and enterprise — or APE for short.

Crossing genres to explore an even darker side of campus life was Helen Garner's *The First Stone* about sexual harassment in a student college.

Movies and television have followed, with the lawn at the University of Melbourne welcoming mature-age student Jack Thompson in *Peterson*, the underground carpark doubling as a hide-out in the first *Mad Max* film, and the arts faculty providing a backdrop to Emma-Kate Croghan's delightful *Love and Other Catastrophes*.

For many viewers though, their image of a university was formed by watching the immensely popular *Brideshead Revisited*, with its soft-focus shots of undergraduate life at an enchanted Oxford early in the 1920s, a world of teddy bears, smart tailoring, expensive champagne, languid afternoons and remarkably little study.

Brideshead was as compelling in Australia as in Britain — an echo perhaps of lingering Australian attachment to British ideals of university life. Australian expatriate Clive James recalled this insecurity from his university days in Sydney. 'The university motto,' he wrote, 'was *sidere mens eadem mutato*, which loosely translated means "Sydney University is really Oxford or Cambridge laterally displaced approximately 12,000 miles."'

A more literal rendition might suggest 'though the constellations change, the mind is universal'. And Clive James, like generations of Australian memoirists, understood how much he gained from time on campus. Pen in hand, James took extensive notes, covering in his first year English, modern history, psychology and anthropology. For James, each course raised more questions than he could answer. But 'my pen raced on, unhampered by the mind's doubts,' he recalled.

This constant cultural output reflects the rich comic potential of campus life, but an equally strong commitment to the ideal of higher education. For academic novelists, universities are vital, essential places — worth lampooning, deserving targets for polemic.

The contemporary university is a place like no other, full of brilliant, passionate and independent-minded people. It is not for the faint-hearted. One study of university leadership quotes a colleague who, in a previous life, had been a soldier. He remarks that:

> ... in the army, we used to argue like mad, but when the decision was made, that was it: 100 per cent focus on getting the job done.
> In a university, by contrast, when the decision is made it seems to signal the starting gun for the debate to

commence in earnest, using all the "political" weapons at people's disposal!

The army at least has an enemy to fight. We have only ourselves.

Elaborate rituals of negotiation become a familiar part of the culture. Setting the annual budget is a process that takes months every year. In one university rather well known to me, this lengthy negotiation between deans and central administration culminates in a three-day live-in conference where forty-five members of the campus community finally and exhaustively lay to rest the minute details of where next year's money goes.

And yet Australian universities are far more efficient places than might be supposed. They do much with little. The creative energy born of dissidence, debate, high degrees of specialisation and the sheer intelligence of the group constantly amazes — innovation, breakthroughs in research, great teaching and learning, and a steady flow of ideas into our wider democracy. As in the city states of Athens, Rome and Florence, the modern republic of learning thrives on competition for acclaim.

Given the strange blend of technical skills and persuasion involved in running universities, managers in the sector must call on an unusual combination of talents. Public universities in Australia now raise most of their own funds, so some ability to manage revenue is an unavoidable priority.

But financial skills alone are not enough. The university leader also needs enthusiasm for diversity, for managing the endlessly creative, and simply for sympathising with a subculture possessing sharp minds and sharper pens.

* * *

Universities are places where the citizens pride themselves on an independence of mind. Though universities compete vigorously against each other for students and research funds, the academy is impressed neither by the apparatus of marketing nor by claims to modern management. They work within, and value, a collegial republic.

Such tensions around the role of management on campus offer a familiar international story. One of the great educational visionaries was Clark Kerr. As leader of the University of California Berkeley, Kerr designed the Californian university system. It was Kerr's proud boast that no qualified student was ever turned away from a Californian state university under his watch.

Kerr believed a university should protect academic freedom. For this, he paid a high price. As the Free Speech Movement grew up around Berkeley in 1964, Kerr found himself caught between students demanding a greater voice in the university and a conservative governing board, which felt the university was already too accommodating. When Ronald Reagan became governor of California in 1967, after promising he would 'clean up the mess in Berkeley', Clark Kerr was dismissed from office.

Kerr did not lose his wit as he received his marching orders: 'I leave as I arrived,' he announced. 'Fired with enthusiasm!'

Free speech is an honoured tradition at Australian universities too. Every major campus in every Australian state witnesses scenes of tumult at some time. When amateur student thespian Gough Whitlam was dismissed as prime minister by the governor-general in 1975, thousands of students walked off campuses around the nation. In 1976, the Australian Union of Students organised a national day of action against plans by the Fraser government to bring in fees for some courses. Students were among the first to take up the argument against apartheid, environmental degradation, war and discrimination, often long before such causes found a wider audience.

Yet as Alice Garner writes in *The Student Chronicles*, student protest has never seemed the same since the battle over HECS was lost, around 1989. Garner noted that by the mid 1990s, students had become so disengaged from campus politics most only voted when bribed with free food.

Nonetheless, passions were stirred by long-running battles over voluntary student unionism in the final years of the Howard government. Issues still remain that can ignite student anger. Concerns over the safety of Indian students in Melbourne during 2009 led to a sit-down protest on Flinders Street.

Many graduates look back on their protesting days with justified pride. Speaking out against discrimination, making the case for social justice, should be part of the university experience — whether or not they appear on the curriculum.

Alongside protest is a great tradition of theatre and performance. Universities have spawned numerous actors, journalists, writers and directors. Barry Humphries tried law, philosophy and fine arts at university before realising it was performance that inspired him. David Williamson began studying engineering at Monash before finding his metier as a playwright.

As Rob Sitch, one of the talented graduates behind *The Hollowmen*, *Frontline* and *The Castle*, observed: 'There is a great myth about universities that you go there to learn about chemistry and physics, but that is all rubbish. It is the farting around in between that you learn things from.' Many a university revue has been the first step in a long career.

Student newspapers are important in the tradition of free speech on campus. For generations, papers with memorable titles such as *Honi Soit*, *Farrago*, *Rabelais*, *Tharunka*, *Lot's Wife*, *Crossfire*, *Semper Floreat*, *Quasimodo* and — perhaps most suggestive of all, *Grapeshot* — have voiced the student challenge to conventional wisdom and the way universities are run.

Likewise student politics have been a training ground for future leaders. Robert Menzies was first elected to office as president of the Students' Representative Council at the University of Melbourne. He would return, fifty years later, as chancellor. Harold Holt was president of the University Law Students' Society. Julia Gillard served as president of the National Union of Students, while Liberal leader Tony Abbott earned his political spurs as a conservative student activist.

In *Battlelines*, Abbott recalls: 'In 1979 I became president of the Sydney University Students' Representative Council. In the campaign I recall getting a good cheer when I promised to replace the SRC's Che Guevara posters with a portrait of the Queen. There was an even bigger one for promising to install a portrait of the Pope!'

Campus provides a safe place to learn politics — a chance to try out ideas, develop speaking skills, lead a large student union, or get elected to council on a platform of idealism.

* * *

Among university leaders, nobody has written with more wisdom than Berkeley's Clark Kerr about the purposes of a university and the trials of leading such a lively, argumentative institution.

As an economist, Kerr suggested we understand these extraordinary places as a multiversity — a series of diverse organisational units and individuals held together only, he quipped, by a common grievance over parking.

He might have used instead the metaphor of the classic republican state, in which power is divided between institutions and individuals. In the republic, no one person can acquire sufficient authority to dictate decisions. Governance must be shared — and while this makes conflict inevitable, it also provides rules by which disagreement can be debated and resolved.

To an outsider, this idea of shared government can seem counterintuitive. Management structures in corporations reflect a classic hierarchy — the board of directors holds legal power, executive action is taken by the CEO and management team, and the workers report to the management.

Not so at any Australian university. Here, as the shrewd manager knows, decisions without widespread support will be contested — or passively resisted.

Across the university's many divides, between administrators and academics, between deans and schools, the arts and science, the research and the teaching agenda, sometimes even between staff and students, ample opportunity exists for dispute and disagreement.

On a daily basis, citizens of the republic of learning take enthusiastic advantage of this opportunity.

Once campus was a gentle place
now education's a ruthless race.
If clarion call comes from afar
we'll fight to defend G's Wine Bar.

So raise the scarlet standard high
and praise our university.
Our trademark stands above the fray
the red flag flies on open day.

As in the classic republic, so in universities. Authority is held collectively by the academic body, represented through an academic board or senate. Serious matters are discussed in formal venues and the university bar alike.

Individual academics are accorded freedom to control their own curriculum and research, and to speak publicly about their area of expertise. Governance proceeds by committee and consultation.

And when a leader is required, it must be a fellow citizen. University vice-chancellors, the closest to a CEO these organisations allow, are selected almost exclusively from the ranks of teaching and researching academics.

Thus scientists and humanities scholars, nurses and engineers, economists and doctors, trained for a life of reflection, scholarship and teaching, find themselves running billion-dollar enterprises.

This pattern of leadership is repeated around the world. Indeed, in many European and Asian universities, the rector is elected by academics, and only for a very short term, so ensuring little executive power to make major change.

As Clark Kerr demonstrated, tenure for a leader can be uncertain too in the United States. Many Australian vice-chancellors likewise come to grief. Formal authority only works if persuasion secures continued support from above and below.

In his memorable formulation, Kerr noted the impossibility of meeting every aspect of the role:

> The university president in the United States is expected to be a friend of the students, a colleague of the faculty, a good fellow with the alumni, a sound administrator with the trustees, a good speaker with the public, an astute bargainer with the foundations and the federal agencies, a politician with the state legislature, a friend of industry, labor and agriculture, a persuasive diplomat with donors, a champion of education generally, a supporter of the professions (particularly law and

medicine), a spokesman to the press, a scholar in his own right, a public servant at the state and national levels, a devotee of opera and football equally, a decent human being, a good husband and father, an active member of a church. Above all he must enjoy travelling in airplanes, eating his meals in public, and attending public ceremonies. No one can be all of these things. Some succeed at being none.

In this wonderful quote, Kerr writes as though university leaders are inevitably men, but women now count prominently among Australia's most successful vice-chancellors. And such vice-chancellors must perform their prescribed role in a university culture that sees leadership as a regrettable necessity.

The organisation they lead is an improbable amalgam, an overlapping set of teaching, research and knowledge-transfer responsibilities. The university is a major property holder, large employer, important contributor to the local economy, a big organisation that seeks to mix traditional structures (academic boards, summer breaks) with the stark realities of market vulnerability and endless competition. Being in senior management at a university, noted one deputy vice-chancellor, is like spending your life in a casino — day and night, you're stuck there in front of a screen.

* * *

Leadership in a university is a partnership with a large, young population. The university is very much about young people learning, researching, discovering themselves and the world. It is a culture of student newspapers, theatre, satire, protests that shut down the administration for an hour or two, alongside the quiet work of helping students who fall on hard times.

Universities are not institutions that need a justification to be articulated by a chief executive, nor even a constant reminder of purpose. In the republic of learning, universities serve many important aspirations, with all the incoherence that implies.

The tradition of free expression means those in a university are encouraged to question. They can chase serious topics and they can mock. They can debate fiercely where the apostrophe should rest in a passage to be named 'Professor's walk'. For these are places of dazzling and committed people, who can parody their institution on the one hand, and remain fiercely loyal to the ideal on the other.

The mood has darkened recently as public funding has tightened further. Financial pressure has carried into university life unwelcome performance measures and an end to the tenure system that once guaranteed jobs. These are now fragile institutions, dependent on foreign markets and the next research grant, prone to the insecurities of uncertain support.

In his 1996 Boyer lectures, China scholar Pierre Ryckmans joked that universities in Australia no longer actually exist: they have become like the stage props used in Peking Opera, where a sign that says 'This is a castle' or 'This is a forest' takes the place of background scenery.

The modern Australian university has moved so far from the classic ideal, concluded Professor Ryckmans, we might as well just herd the students and teachers into an ordinary city office building and put a sign out front saying: 'This is a university.'

Pierre Ryckmans quotes British journalist Malcolm Muggeridge, who believed the main reason people look at universities with a certain feeling of awe is because so few actually have access to them. When more people know what universities are really like, suggested Muggeridge, their prestige may fall to virtually nil.

In Australia, university study is more popular than ever. If a test of esteem is the desire to join, universities have never been held in higher standing. Yet this enthusiasm has not flowed through to the broader community. People who work on campus know there remains something special about the scholarly life, a sense that every day of the week outstanding academics across every discipline engage with young people to share and advance knowledge.

But they do so in trying circumstances. Funding per student declines while student numbers increase. Staff–student ratios have moved from twelve to one to more than twenty to one.

Beyond the university gates, concern about overload has found little sympathy. While a passionate minority advocate fervently for universities, and most Australians want a first-class education for their children, university policy has not proved a vote-switching issue. Despite the efforts of the sector, election after election, higher education fails to register.

This raises an intriguing question: is the sector's frequent inability to attract political attention a sign of weakness — or an unwelcome effect of success?

On one hand, many citizens of the republic of learning lament the attention lavished on hospitals and roads by politicians every election. Why do they never seek office by promising more support for universities, particularly now all federal ministers have university qualifications themselves?

The traditional answer to this baffling indifference seems simple: there are no votes in higher education. Perhaps this will change when 40 per cent of young Australians attend university in the near future.

But on the other hand, the profile for higher education in national politics may tell a different story. Despite adversity, universities have proved resilient. Faced with funding cuts, they found new income sources by attracting international students. Required to accommodate more Australian students, they have expanded. The campuses that dot our cities and towns appear large, growing and prosperous. No public university has gone broke in decades, and despite occasional governance crises, universities are not seen as at risk. We can be safely left alone.

It would be unfortunate if it required a major disaster to awaken public interest in institutions that contribute to the prosperity of every community.

And yet ... as a way to organise self-motivated individuals, to group like-minded people into areas of disciplinary strength, and to encourage pure research and exciting innovation, universities remain an institution worth more than passing interest.

For all the good-humoured ribbing, some of the most innovative companies now emulate the university form — clustering their researchers onto a campus, providing time for individual research, recognising that innovation is not a linear process but requires a loosely controlled organisation with plenty of room for personal eccentricity and informal discussion.

In a world in which information is endless, and key messages must be shared, debated and then acted upon, the structure and ethos of a university proves remarkably adept. Like good republics, universities strengthen amid flux and disagreement. It is a sign of their virtue.

Dedicated to the teaching and refinement of knowledge, universities are the original information organisation. Today they find themselves with a new relevance. Business commentator Gary Hamel remarks: 'Anyone who has ever run a university, a film studio or an open source project will tell you that getting the most out of people seldom means managing them more, and usually means managing them less.'

Universities, like the republics of Machiavelli's day, inject something new and important into the bloodstream of surrounding societies. Universities can be hard to govern, but like the cities Machiavelli praised, they understand it is 'the common good, and not private gain' that makes communities great. This sense of purpose helps universities produce extraordinary energy, new knowledge and innovation.

Despite the challenges, the heartache at times, the intense internal gaze, the university has proved adept at retaining its traditional form, even as it cloaks itself in contemporary garb. It has endured by recognising that everything must change so that everything can stay the same.

Or as the Chancellors of Vice sang about Griffith University …

The Republic of Learning

Beneath our emblem proudly stand
resolved to ne'er dilute the brand
if anything makes us smarter still,
the scarlet emblem surely will.

> *So raise the scarlet standard high*
> *and praise our university.*
> *Our trademark stands above the fray*
> *the red flag flies on open day.*

Six
The Republic of Learning

Look at those stone gates, the passing parade of youth, the staff hurrying between classrooms. From the right distance the university seems eternal, barely changing with the centuries.

In many countries, including Australia, universities are among the oldest continually operating organisations — part of an international republic of learning stretching back over half a millennium.

This is a remarkable feat. Very few institutions survive so long. In the western world the only surviving entities from 1520, in recognisable form with similar functions and unbroken histories, include the Catholic Church, the parliaments of the Isle of Man, of Iceland and of Great Britain, several Swiss cantons, the Bank of Siena — and seventy universities.

This longevity is made possible by the importance of their mission — teaching the next generation — and by a healthy capacity for adaptation. In Australia the women once excluded from campus now make up a majority of students. Campuses once speaking only to locals now educate hundreds of thousands of students from Asia. A workforce once dependent on muscle now finds roles for 170,000 graduates each year. A nation that imported scientific knowledge now contributes in a significant way to the global expansion of learning.

Australia's university system is one of our great achievements, a key to our continued prosperity.

Throughout this book we have examined our republic of learning — developments in teaching, research, social equity and life on campus. The state of the republic is strong, even if there remains much to be done in providing more universal access.

But every institution can be better, stronger, more relevant. So in this final chapter I want to ask whether we are taking full advantage of the potential benefits offered by higher learning.

Donald Horne was being ironic when he called us the lucky country. Yet the phrase stuck in a nation benefiting from the economic miracle of a sustained mining boom. We've enjoyed decades of continuous growth and our living standards have been lifted remarkably. With the combination of hard work and the scientific, engineering and financial expertise provided by higher education, we have turned the red dust of the Pilbara into the steel, copper and energy that is building and powering cities across the globe.

Will this economic luck last? Let's hope so — and in directions compatible with a fragile ecosystem.

It is common to fret that an economy based on just one

industry will always be vulnerable. Yet over the past twenty years we have invented another huge new sector in Australia, something to sit alongside mining as a fundamental pillar of prosperity.

Higher education is our largest service export, among our largest employers. It provides the skills to turn prosperity generated by the red dust into something else — a store of intellect and skills, of creative energy that will power our nation in the years ahead.

Higher education has attracted some of the most talented people from our region to study here. And about a third choose to stay in Australia as permanent residents. We are all the richer for their contribution. Turning promising material into extraordinary people is the practical chemistry higher education offers. Given the scale of the opportunity, it's time to think big.

In 2009 the Australian government responded to the Bradley Review of Higher Education by setting the nation a series of challenges: to ensure 40 per cent of twenty-five- to thirty-four-year-olds have a bachelors degree or higher by 2025, to make our higher education system more equitable, and to keep standards high.

Expanding access is an important goal, and one likely to be achieved. Participation is already at 34 per cent and growing strongly.

But the numbers of new students involved require some bold decisions. To take in an additional 360,000 or more students means we will need a significant number of new universities around the nation — up to twenty-four new institutions over the next twenty years suggests one estimate from noted analyst Mike Gallagher.

We can do this. Our higher education system has expanded significantly in recent decades and can manage again. The experience of the past gives us a strong base for further growth.

But as another period of rapid expansion looms, now is the time to ask how best to imagine these new students and new universities. Growth provides an opportunity to enlarge the diversity of higher education in Australia.

Today Australia relies on one model to achieve its higher education goals — the Australian public university. Shaped by funding policies and regulation, our public universities have much in common. They all aspire to be research universities, with research now written into the legal definition of a university. They all offer courses in a wide array of disciplines, and degree levels from bachelor to PhD. They are all large, with an average of 27,000 students each, usually spread over several campuses. All have similar administrative structures, with faculties, academic boards, governing councils or senates, and vice-chancellors.

This was not planned. On the contrary, at various times policymakers have sought to encourage a far more varied range of institutions.

What is now the University of New South Wales (UNSW) began in 1949 as the New South Wales University of Technology, intended to be a science and engineering institution. Monash University too was designed to specialise in similar disciplines. But the moment was lost. Rapid expansion, and an urgent need for graduates from all disciplines saw UNSW and

Monash quickly become comprehensive institutions, with course offerings and academic missions resembling closely the original universities in Sydney and Melbourne.

From the 1960s a new generation of universities began, with the establishment of Macquarie, La Trobe, Newcastle, Flinders, Griffith, Wollongong and Murdoch. Once again the original plans called for institutions that embraced interdisciplinary knowledge, with innovative courses that complemented rather than repeated the offerings of existing universities.

It was not to last. Again, the pressure for rapid growth, and a concern to capture students interested primarily in professional training, saw all this generation of universities become comprehensive. Today they provide professional schools in medicine, business, law and engineering, of very high quality and eerie familiarity.

In the late 1980s, the federal government met continued pressure for university places by a massive process of consolidation. A range of once independent and distinctive teaching institutions — colleges of advanced education, institutes of technology and sundry specialist schools — were remade as universities.

This process of amalgamation heralded the age of the mega-university. Australia's universities remain much bigger on average than counterparts in Britain, where universities average 15,000 students, or Japan with just 4000 students on average.

Within the newly amalgamated universities, powerful forces of standardisation and uniformity set to work. Academics with a masters degree and a lifelong commitment to teaching found

themselves no longer welcome. To secure research grants —
the currency of academic prestige — universities now only
employed scholars with a doctorate. As research became the
basis of rankings, so Australian universities narrowed around
this single mission.

Amalgamation proved a way to expand places for students
without increasing government outlays. The 1990s saw a
steady decline in public funding per student. Class sizes
increased to create economies of scale. Universities turned to
international students in ever greater numbers to cover the
widening gap between income and costs.

The reforms of the late 1980s deserve credit for expanding
dramatically the opportunities for young Australians to attend
university. But such growth was achieved at the price of
sameness, in what was labelled a unified national system.
Regulation would enforce conformity. All universities would
have a research mission. Indeed universities would be funded
to be alike, so that the experience of attending Edith Cowan
University's Joondalup campus in Perth should be instantly
familiar to a student at any of the seven campuses of Charles
Sturt University in regional New South Wales.

Given this similarity, it is little wonder so few Australian
students cross state borders to study — wherever they go, the
courses on offer will be much the same. Uniformity means
consistency, and students can have confidence in the quality
of their course, wherever they study, but the cost is a lack of
meaningful choice.

Twenty years after the period of great amalgamation
enforced a single model for an Australian university, there is a

mood for change. This arises from universities themselves, which are keen to develop a distinct identity and respond to changing student expectations.

Canberra too shows a new interest in diversity. The 2008 Bradley Review recommended less prescriptive regulation, more opportunity for higher education institutions to develop their own character.

In response, the Commonwealth has announced major changes to the funding system. From 2012 universities can now choose how many students to enrol — a decision that will create, overnight, tens of thousands of additional places for Australian students. Canberra will step back from direct regulation of universities, relying instead on an independent authority to ensure minimum standards and quality.

It is a welcome development, one that encourages institutions to experiment more boldly with curriculum.

Universities are moving quickly to broaden their education model, to develop courses that offer an expansive view of humanity and its environment. Such education aims to create citizens, along with preparing students for the workforce. It makes clear that while universities transmit skills, they also give us a reason to ponder the purpose of life.

The aim is to encourage rounded human beings, who question and who understand. At the University of Melbourne, major change to undergraduate education began in 2008. Ninety-six separate programs became six undergraduate degree programs, each marked by compulsory 'breadth components' to ensure every Melbourne undergraduate studies subjects outside their choice of degree program. Science students can now explore music as part of their program, and commerce students languages. Melbourne aims, like other Australian universities, to encourage a distinctive kind of graduate, one with breadth as well as depth.

Undergraduate study then leads to a wide array of graduate programs. At Melbourne, and from 2012 at the University of Western Australia, professional courses such as law, medicine, teaching and engineering will only be taught at graduate level. Students have time to explore their many interests before committing to intensive graduate training, taught with the rigour appropriate to masters-level programs.

This move, dubbed 'the Melbourne Model' by *The Age* newspaper, offers an education aligned to European and North American practice. It has been supported by both sides of politics when in government, by funding Commonwealth-supported places in graduate courses.

Other universities will make their own decisions about strategy. On campus, as in Canberra, policy has begun to favour diversity — a wider set of choices for Australian students.

The important next step will be a review, due in 2011, to examine the funding rate for each course.

At present there is a strange double nature to our public universities. Regulation requires that Australian students be offered a strictly enforced uniformity, with standardised pricing and largely similar products. These sit alongside an open market for international students and Australian postgraduates, who are free to choose their degree according to quality, reputation and cost, as they would any other serious investment in their future.

Addressing this curious dual arrangement is the crucial next reform. Until the funding for each course reflects real costs, no university can afford to specialise.

Take the study of law. An Australian undergraduate student in law attracts a Commonwealth subsidy of just $1800 a year. The student pays a further $9000. But in most institutions the real cost of delivering quality legal programs is many thousands of dollars a year more. The financial gap is filled by income from international and private full-fee-paying students.

This creates a serious risk: when international enrolments fall, so does international revenue. This creates a difficult choice for our public universities — to reduce the quality of courses or to maintain quality at the cost of reducing the number of places available to Australian students.

Underfunding in some disciplines, such as law, requires large enrolments in other subjects such as business to generate sufficient income to support the overall institution.

The diversity agenda, therefore, relies on funding the real cost of a university education. There is a case for significant additional public investment and for thinking again about the private contribution.

Funding the full cost of research is crucial also to establishing a more diverse higher education sector. Currently, funding for research only covers a part of the actual cost of research. The gap must be made up by cross-subsidising research from other funding sources. In particular, universities use income from teaching, or allow existing infrastructure to degrade, to instead support research programs. The more successful the research programs of a university, the greater the cost to teaching and buildings.

To cope with rapid expansion, government will likely look beyond the existing thirty-seven public universities. Australia has two private universities — Bond and Notre Dame — and 137 other institutions registered to offer higher education courses. These include theological colleges, professional bodies such as the Institute of Chartered Accountants, natural medicine colleges, and a variety of specialised training academies. A small number of TAFEs also offer undergraduate degrees.

Yet, taken together, these bodies account for only 6 per cent of all higher education enrolments. The overwhelming majority of degree students, some 94 per cent, are enrolled in our public universities.

Hopefully this reflects the high standing and prestige of public universities. But it is likely cost is also a factor since, with a handful of minor exceptions, direct subsidy of higher education is limited to public universities. The average subsidy across all disciplines in public universities is $11,000 per student per year. This gives public universities a major competitive advantage.

This sharp difference between public and private contrasts with the more varied systems found elsewhere. In the United States, India and China, governments encourage higher education institutions to specialise by field or level of study.

In the United States, a large private higher education sector adds greatly to the options on offer. Millions of students are enrolled in one of more than 2000 private higher education institutions, most focused on teaching rather than research.

American students embrace this choice. Many choose to study interstate, at the campus that best reflects their particular interests. An aspiring novelist, for instance, may prefer a small liberal arts college such as Wellesley. A potential astronomer may choose MIT, an ambitious banker a business program at Northwestern University.

This choice does come at a price — sometimes hundreds of thousands of dollars in fees, to be paid up front or through a loan. Australians put a greater premium on egalitarian outcomes, and many will feel the American system is purchased at too high a level of social inequality.

Yet recent developments in the American market provide important indications of the way higher education is changing.

Consider the rise of Phoenix University, one of America's for-profit institutions. Calling itself a 'university for working adults', Phoenix offers a range of vocationally focused associate, bachelor, masters and doctoral courses. These can be studied online and through 265 local 'learning centres'. From a small college offering correspondence courses, Phoenix now enrols more than 440,000 students and employs 25,000 instructors.

Phoenix has refined a business model that ruthlessly eliminates costs irrelevant to the outcomes its students seek. Phoenix academics are not paid to do research, but they do have to mark student papers within forty-eight hours of submission. Classes contain no more than fifteen students. By renting space in office buildings and shopping centres, Phoenix avoids investment in expensive campus infrastructure — the sandstone, cloisters, and gargoyles of a traditional university are nowhere to be found. And half Phoenix's offerings are associate degrees. These provide a way into higher education for students not qualified for, or ready to commit to, longer bachelor degrees.

To some, these qualities make Phoenix a poor imitation of the traditional university. But if you cannot spare four years out of work to spend on campus, and you need a qualification to get a better job, Phoenix can give you higher education at a far cheaper price, and with much greater convenience.

Ready or not, it's a model coming to a country near you.

The idea of education for profit sits uncomfortably with the ethos of Australia's public universities and it can be controversial in the United States too; a recent US Government Accountability Office audit identified 'fraudulent, deceptive or otherwise questionable marketing practices' in the sector.

Yet the rapid growth and large enrolments of the American for-profit institutions suggest we should think carefully about why they appeal to so many students. Perhaps it is because the American for-profit education industry provides a pathway for students who otherwise struggle. Not every public institution works to meet the needs of working adults.

Similar institutions are gaining a foothold in Australia. The stock-market-listed Navitas group runs diploma-granting colleges that prepare students for university entry, offering small classes and close involvement with teachers. Navitas colleges are often situated on campus so students get comfortable about eventually joining the university. If they complete their diploma courses with sufficient marks, Navitas students can enter the second year of a university course.

We think of opening access as the special task of public education. Yet public universities have not always proved well matched to this challenge. Some have resolved this dilemma by establishing close working partnerships with Navitas or its competitors. Some have established their own feeder colleges. Other public universities talk of establishing community colleges on the American and British model, offering two-year associate degrees with articulation into further study.

Closer links between universities and Australia's well-established network of TAFE institutes offer a further opportunity for greater diversity. Around a dozen TAFEs provide university-style courses, often with an exit point after the second year for those not keen to continue to a degree. The network of TAFE colleges, especially in regional areas, enables them to reach students who cannot travel to a university campus but may not want to study online.

For those attracted to distance study, Open Universities Australia, now affiliated with Seek Learning, offers access to online courses from fourteen public universities, including a growing suite of masters-level courses.

As universities such as Melbourne and Western Australia move to a graduate school model, they may leave an opening for new undergraduate-only institutions, in the tradition of America's liberal arts colleges. Australia currently has only one — Campion College in Western Sydney. We could do with more.

Liberal arts colleges believe in a university as a place of scholarship and reflection, free from the pressing imperatives of career choice for students. They remain close to the humanist aspirations of the first global scholar, Erasmus. Such colleges account for only a small percentage of total enrolments in the United States, but places are highly sought after, and satisfaction rates from students tend to be very high.

The attractions are obvious: small residential campuses, the feeling of a community in which every face is recognisable, comfortable class sizes, with teaching provided by professors not faced with the constant pressure to publish.

A good example is Williams College in Massachusetts, where all students must take subjects across the three divisions of language and arts, social studies, and science and mathematics. The idea is to create broadly educated graduates, familiar with different ways of understanding the world, well qualified to enrol in professional graduate programs such as law and medicine. There are no vocational courses offered.

Alongside liberal arts colleges in the United States are hundreds of specialist institutions, with most in health, technology, music and the arts, law and theology. Perhaps the most famous is the California Institute of Technology (Caltech), which specialises in engineering, science, maths and astronomy. Caltech has places for only 2000 students, but remains one of America's most successful higher education institutions, with thirty-one of its staff or alumni winning Nobel prizes.

Such achievements may be an exception rather than the norm, but an undivided focus on a small set of related disciplines can produce excellence.

The American example of the small specialist institution

is matched by the Indian institutes of management and technology, by Chinese universities focused on engineering or aviation, by the Singapore Management University, or by Lingnan University, a small but vibrant liberal arts college in Hong Kong. With just 2500 students, almost exclusively undergraduates, Lingnan has introduced a welcome diversity into Hong Kong's higher education system. Its senior academic staff include renowned professors such as Australian Meaghan Morris, who spends time in Hong Kong with students keen for an education in the humanities before considering graduate school or career and professional options.

Many Lingnan graduates choose a business career, alongside those who work in the arts or media — a source of satisfaction for Lingnan staff, who see their mission as shaping well-educated and well-rounded individuals who will make a contribution in all fields.

With relatively few universities, how will Australia provide more choice for students?

In part the answer lies in rethinking regulation and funding. Canberra can still treat all public institutions in an even-handed way, while providing scope and encouragement for each university to find its own path, play to its own strengths and build distinctive expertise in specialist fields.

In part the path to diversity is to use imminent expansion of the system to introduce new types of institutions. It will be hard to accommodate so many new students in existing universities. Why not create some new players consciously different — Australian liberal arts colleges, specialist academies, community colleges and whatever entirely new organisations are made possible by a national broadband network and the ability to aggregate content from universities around the world?

The answer involves more mobility for students, and recognising that a new generation will want to move between institutions, classrooms and online courses, building their own study programs.

And in part diversity requires us to rethink the sharp public/private divide of our education world. This is already happening, as TAFEs and private providers attract fee-paying degree students. But Canberra mandates maximum charges for Australian undergraduates, which limits competition on price between public institutions.

And, as Navitas demonstrates, it is possible to draw students into a private course that leads to public university study. Such close alliances between public and private will only grow as the nation strives to achieve its targets for participation in higher education.

But to work effectively, we need to think again about the allocation of Commonwealth-supported places and the operation of HECS.

Finally, we need to consider ways that gifted teachers can be part of a university system that is currently built around research. There are many universities that will remain utterly committed to their research mission and workforce — and so they should. But it must be possible to create opportunities for those scholars at their best in the classroom with students, teachers who keep up with the literature without themselves researching. We waste so much talent through our narrow definition of what it means to be a university.

New forms of regulation will be required for each of these changes, but they are not conceptually difficult. Rather, the impediment is deep cultural assumptions about what it means to be a university.

That most famous book on the subject, Cardinal Newman's classic *The Idea of a University*, proclaimed a singular vision of higher education — not *an* idea but *the* idea of a university. Like Newman, Australia has only tolerated *one* idea of what a university should be. In an era of mass education, a republic of learning needs to re-imagine the prevailing archetype of the university, opening up to new types of institutions, new ways of thinking about higher education.

This is not about titles. It matters little what a great higher education institute is called. Nobody in the United States confuses Phoenix University with Harvard. MIT is not called a university, but few miss its contribution to the world of ideas. Real difference is found not in labels but in the issues at the heart of these lectures: teaching, research, equity and life on campus.

Our republic of learning should encourage more dual-sector vocational and higher education institutions, and more specialised universities, liberal arts schools and small colleges committed to their own subject area, their own vision of higher education.

We cannot expect the public to fund every experiment in higher education. It is reasonable for government to specify what types of courses and students it will support. Governments are entitled to fund new students beginning their career at one rate, and already established professionals at another. But as a nation we have to meet the needs of all potential students in a way that is fair, equitable and affordable.

There are important debates ahead about which disciplines need public support. Once decisions are made, they should apply equally to all students and all institutions.

What is not funded by government must be funded privately, through student fees and philanthropy. Australia has a superb record in lending students money to cover their fees, while exempting students and graduates with low earnings from repayment. It is a model that can be extended to other modes of education, and to providing reasonable living costs while studying.

By expanding choice and by supporting students we create the best possible opportunity for each Australian to access the education they value, and to contribute to its costs later, as they benefit from the qualification.

To achieve diversity, we need to make the student fee and loan system flexible for all students, so they can make their own decisions about how much to invest in their higher education.

And we need to encourage the continued flow of international students — to build the intellectual resources of this nation, to ensure an Australia that faces outwards and finds its place in the region.

The consequences of opening up the system are hard to predict. The trickle of foreign higher education institutions entering Australia — Laureate International, Study Group, Kaplan Professional, the Adelaide campuses of Carnegie-Mellon University and University College London — may become a steady stream of new arrivals if the funding system puts them on equal footing in appealing to students.

But just as important is allowing older institutions to re-invent themselves. For the foreseeable future, public universities will educate the vast majority of Australian higher education students. Each must be encouraged to find the future that works best for them.

Fortunately, universities are inventive institutions. When our public universities needed to find new sources of income, they invented an international student industry. That same spirit of innovation can be harnessed again. Government does not need to mandate diversity — by making regulation only about standards, diversity will follow. Each public university, determined to make its way in the world, will invent the future that makes sense for it and its communities.

Where the government can most help build the republic of learning is where universities cannot act alone. Without a successful education revolution in early childhood, our university students will still reflect too narrow a slice of Australian society.

We have in our midst an array of institutions committed to higher education, filled with great minds, devoted to teaching, engagement and research. They serve the public and deserve support in return. Research in particular is expensive and risky; promising ideas do not always turn out as hoped. Only public funding can sustain the research effort needed to widen our understanding of the world and to enrich lives.

Our universities compete and connect, collaborate and vigorously contend, but each makes Australia a better place.

Universities will shape the next generation and sustain our shared prosperity and our national conversation. Our future lies not just under our soil but in our minds and our hands. In this moment of knowledge, of technology, of skills and of the global movement of peoples, Australia needs to be a vigorous participant in the worldwide republic of learning.

It's a historic moment. The promise of a door kicked open 500 years ago by Erasmus and the republic of letters finds a contemporary echo. While search engines, Wikipedia and Facebook offer information on demand, it requires higher education to make something of their endless data — and their promise of sustained knowledge for every individual who seeks it, for every community, and for humanity. Australia is part of this moment, and it can help lead.

Thanks to a lively and engaged higher education system, we embrace the ambition Erasmus set us — *Ego mundi civis esse cupio* — to be citizens of the world, citizens of this republic of learning.

Acknowledgements

With thanks to Chairperson Maurice Newman AC and the directors of the Australian Broadcasting Corporation for the invitation to present this series of lectures.

Suzanne Donisthorpe provided guidance and helpful suggestions as she produced the series for Radio National. Thanks also to Garry Havrillay at ABC Studios, Southbank, Melbourne, and Susan Morris-Yates from ABC Books.

This work was undertaken with fond memories of the late Richard Boyer — son of the ABC leader commemorated by this lecture series, and himself a member of the first Corporation board from 1983. As a doctoral student at the ANU, I watched Richard develop his thinking about the role of public broadcasting. Marion Consandine notes in her excellent entry in the *Australian Dictionary of Biography* that Richard Boyer urged the ABC to expand the 'range of ideas, interests and experiences available to the whole Australian community'.

My thanks also to Chancellor Alex Chernov and colleagues at the University of Melbourne for their good grace and patience while I worked on this text.

In particular I am keen to acknowledge the enthusiastic team who contributed so much to the project — Gwilym Croucher, Dennis Glover, Paul Gray, Shane Huntington,

Andrew Norton and Sam Rosevear. Our work together included an intranet site to share information, a spreadsheet to track mention of particular institutions, endless trading of drafts, and the enjoyment of swapping and debating ideas. I am much in their debt, and any merits in this work reflect their contribution.

Given this generous support from the University of Melbourne, all author fees and royalties from the 2010 Boyer lectures have been donated to supporting Melbourne Access and Equity Scholarships.

Lecture 5 includes 'The Griffith Flag', a track by the Chancellors of Vice recorded in the Griffith University School of Arts Gold Coast studios in December 2004. I appreciate the willingness of fellow band members Patrick Bishop, John 'the Colonel' Campbell, Andrew Fraser and John Kane to allow — indeed cheer — this public outing. Thanks also to Griffith Vice-Chancellor Ian O'Connor for his encouragement.

First drafts of these lectures were written during study leave at the Institute of Education, University of London, in June and July 2010. My thanks to Sir David Watson for arranging the secondment, and to Geoff Mulgan from the Young Foundation for an opportunity to talk over series themes. I appreciated too the hospitality and insights of Don Markwell, Warden of Rhodes House, at Oxford, and a fascinating conversation with Sir Colin Lucas about the nature of instruction — his description of good teaching as 'practical chemistry' resonates still.

A number of people endured long discussions about the ideas in this series, and kindly read and commented on drafts. For the considerable time they invested in advice, suggestions and corrections, and in finding materials or making contacts, I am indebted to Toni Andon, Sanchia Aranda, John Ballard, Graham Brown, Mark Considine, John Dewar, Peter Doherty, Krystal Evans, Michael Gallagher, Jim Gleeson, Richard James, Jane-Frances Kelly, Tom Kvan, Ian Lang, Alan Lawson, Iven Mareels, Ian Marshman, Vin Massaro, Zoë McKenzie, Peter McPhee, Lynn Meek, Gavin Moodie, Frank Moorhouse, Meaghan Morris, Pip Pattison, Bronwen Perry, Peter Rathjen, Jan Reid, Martin Richardson, Field Rickards, Julianne Schultz, Elaine Thompson, Gemma Tunks, Nancy Viviani and Pat Weller.

Simon Marginson from the Centre for the Study of Higher Education generously shared his own work-in-progress on higher education — a chance to compare and contrast manuscripts as we mulled similar topics.

My father, Pedr, and brother, Tony, kindly subedited the manuscript.

Sharon Bell, Sharryn Bowman, Hugh Collins, Amanda Currie, Geoff Sharrock and Laura Trengove put in long hours reading the final draft of the series, and made many valuable suggestions. Nonetheless, they should not be held responsible for the inevitable mistakes and omissions.

Finally, this series is dedicated to Margaret Gardner, not just for characteristically perceptive comments on the manuscript, but for our life together during the twenty-five years we have talked about universities.